OPPORTUNITY FOR LEADERSHIP

OPPORTUNITY FOR LEADERSHIP

Full and Informed Participation

Mark Winston

A Member of the Greenwood Publishing Group

Westport, Connecticut • London

Library of Congress Cataloging-in-Publication Data

Winston, Mark.
Opportunity for leadership : full and informed participation / Mark Winston.
   p. cm.
  Includes bibliographical references and index.
  ISBN 978–1–59158–387–5 (alk. paper)
  1. Political participation—United States. 2. Freedom of information—United
States. I. Title.
  JK1764.W637 2008
  323′.0420973—dc22   2007049030

British Library Cataloguing in Publication Data is available.

Library of Congress Catalog Card Number: 2007049030
ISBN: 978–1–59158–387–5

First published in 2008

Libraries Unlimited, 88 Post Road West, Westport, CT 06881
A Member of the Greenwood Publishing Group, Inc.
www.lu.com

Printed in the United States of America

The paper used in this book complies with the
Permanent Paper Standard issued by the National
Information Standards Organization (Z39.48–1984).

10 9 8 7 6 5 4 3 2 1

Contents

Acknowledgments

The author would like to thank Steve Bahnaman for his research assistance, which contributed to the completion of the book.

Introduction

Opportunity for Leadership: Full and Informed Participation addresses the need for access to information, as well as education, to ensure informed participation in society and informed decision making. While the importance of access is typically described in general terms, the provision of access to information does not automatically enhance learning or facilitate the effective use of information. In addition, access to education as a founding principle of the United States is complicated in origin and has seen evolution in its application over time.

With regard to education, the most frequently identified basis for the plaintiffs' case in *Brown v. Board of Education* is that of fairness and equity; and, the fiftieth anniversary of the Supreme Court decision in 2004 has given it renewed prominence. In Chapter 1, the discussion of the case addresses the fact that the key principle is actually that of access—access to educational opportunities, in particular, and access to full participation in society, in a broader sense. In fact, the selection of education as the context for the first major court case of the modern civil rights era is noteworthy, since access to education became the basis for challenging the system of segregation, while subsequent legislation dealt with access to the political process and civic engagement (the Voting Rights Act) and access to full participation in society (for example, housing, employment, and government contracts). Under the broad rubric of access, then, the challenge of full participation is high-lighted by the complexity of the many issues about which people need to be fully informed.

An informed citizenry, capable of informed participation, is one of the principles on which U.S. democracy is based, with the premise of informed participation represented in Constitutional principles of in-tellectual freedom. However, there have been many attempts to limit access, historically and recently, in relation to information that is con-sidered controversial, with the goal of protecting the individual. Much of this information has been racial or cultural in nature, reflective of current societal context and social issues. Thus, while the controversial is often also the racial, it might be posited that the provision of infor-mation about such circumstances serves to both inform the educational process and ensure that efforts to influence politics and policymaking are informed by the current reality.

So the question becomes whether full and informed participation in the political process and civic engagement requires access to in-formation, representing various viewpoints and perspectives. In some instances, the information is controversial and, being reflective of re-search and/or opinion, may require discernment and analysis. Consis-tent with the principle of intellectual freedom, respect for the individual and taking care that decision making is not controlled by a few high-light the need for ensuring access to information, particularly for the powerless and those whose choices appear to be limited. Thus, Chap-ters 2 and 3 address the value and importance of access to information in a competitive environment and the controversy over access to infor-mation.

Not surprisingly, research related to bias and structural barriers in-dicates that issues of race, ethnicity, and culture, along with language barriers, economic disparities, and geographic isolation limit access to information, including educational opportunities, public and health services, library services, the Internet, and professional choices and op-portunities. All too often, these barriers are erected to limit such access initially, based upon a misplaced desire to protect the vulnerable. What is lost is the importance of the analytical skills and decision making abilities so highly desired by employers in today's information soci-ety but fostered only by the opportunity to evaluate and interpret the usefulness and validity of information in all of its guises.

Efforts to protect various segments of society (children, young adults, and adults) by limiting access to information have seemingly been with us since the dawn of time, whether in books and other publications, broadcast media, or entertainment media or the controversial statements of public figures, individuals, and organizations, including the FCC, volunteer and grassroots organizations, school boards, and publishers. Often the information in question has a racial or cultural focus. In the past, attempts to censor and remove from libraries and K-12 reading lists have included books, such as *Huckleberry Finn*, because of the use of the N-word. More current examples include the selection and labeling of textbooks—curricular decisions by school boards on the basis of religious values, evolution, and homosexuality—and filtering software on library computers.

Both the left and the right censored statements made by Jerry Falwell after 9/11, who blamed certain segments of U.S. society, primarily gays and lesbians and feminists, as the cause of the 9/11 attacks. Add to the discussion efforts to label CDs according to content, the infamous Howard Stern, and the lesser known radio personality Doug Tracht, "The Greaseman," who said "No wonder people drag them behind trucks," following the dragging death of a black man. Finally, consider the ABC advertisement, featuring Terrell Owens and Nicollette Sheridan, which aired before the Monday Night Football game on November 15, 2004, and the 2004 Superbowl Halftime Show, starring Janet Jackson and Justin Timberlake. Both involved an African American and a white protagonist and are largely responsible for much of the enhanced regulation and voluntary censorship in the media.

Young people, from K-12 students, through college-aged individuals and young working adults, to those in the so-called Generation X, are often depicted as both victims of and markets for controversial information, as well as the subject of articulated concern regarding their decision-making ability. At the other end of the spectrum, high-profile cases of successful individuals who have been the subject of ethical investigations dominate public discourse. Thus, the decision-making influences on and processes of young people, especially in the face of such socially charged issues as the death penalty and abortion, are central to the concern related to access to information and effective and informed decision making and are considered in Chapter 4, "An Ethics Crisis." The nature of decision making in the aggregate, as measured by public opinion polls, provides a frame of reference for considering the impact of access to information on the making of these decisions. Subsequently, the nature of the decision-making process of individuals is considered in Chapter 5.

Finally, in terms of providing preparation for full participation in society, the role of agencies such as public libraries and legal defense funds (e.g., the NAACP Legal Defense Fund and the Asian American Legal Defense Fund) must not be overlooked, particularly among those who are disenfranchised. Here too, education plays a leading role in encouraging a greater understanding of and appreciation for sound decision making, as well as offering formal coursework related to leadership, ethics, and civic engagement (Chapter 6). Only then can the populace begin to experience full and informed participation, from which will emerge the leaders of tomorrow.

CHAPTER 1

Brown v. Board of Education and the Constitutional Basis for Access to Information (and Informed Participation)

The case of *Brown v. Board of Education* has been the topic of substantial debate with the recognition of the fiftieth anniversary of the Supreme Court decision in 2004. Some of the discussion has taken the form of celebratory activities; however, scholarly and professional discussions of its meaning, impact, and significance in legal, political, educational, social, and societal terms have highlighted both the importance and the complexity of the decision. Researchers and educators have referred to the pivotal nature of *Brown* as a landmark case, praising the "enormity of [the] decision for the United States in 1954. . . . [and] the significance that it has taken on in the ensuing decades" (Waite 2004, 98) and the understanding of which shedding light on related questions, which will be addressed in greater detail. In many ways, *Brown v. Board of Education* was considered a complex case. Thus, understanding of the case, the perceived and real impact of the Supreme Court decision, and the similar segregation involving other racial and ethnic groups, beyond African Americans, is often of a limited and general nature.

From a historical perspective, the first half of the twentieth century saw the National Association for the Advancement of Colored People (NAACP) determined "to eliminate Jim Crow laws and overturn the doctrine of 'separate but equal,' established in *Plessy v. Ferguson* (1896). Using schools (or educational policy in K-12 settings) as the context, access to education became a rallying call for those challenging the system of segregation that was then in place. It became evident that education would provide the ideal means for challenging these laws" (Waite 2004, 98–99).

Brown v. Board of Education was uniquely positioned to challenge educational inequity and the notion that access to education could be provided with separate facilities. Its complexity can be explained by an analysis of the context of 1954, following three cases which took place in the 1930s and 1940s—*Hocutt v. North Carolina*, *Murray v. University of Maryland Law School*, and, in particular, *Gaines v. Canada* in Missouri:

Lloyd Gaines, a college graduate, had been denied entrance to the law school at the University of Missouri because he was black. Instead, Missouri offered to pay his expenses for law school outside the state. Houston argued that Missouri was obligated to either build a law school for blacks equal to that of whites or admit him to the University of Missouri. The U.S. Supreme Court agreed. (Wormser, 2002)

The final decision reflected a ruling on four individual cases, not only that of Topeka, Kansas. The Supreme Court's determination to rule on four separate cases from four different states of Kansas, South Carolina, Delaware, and Virginia was so described in the published opinion that while they were "premised on different facts and different local conditions,... a common legal question justifies their consideration together in this consolidated opinion." In addition, the justices noted that "[b]ecause of the obvious importance of the question presented, the Court took jurisdiction." Given the limited options for addressing the constitutionality of any issue, the applicability of federal statutes, or the otherwise national significance, just to be heard by the Supreme Court represented a huge step forward in addressing the issues in the case and gaining national exposure. In addition, while Brown, in both intent and outcome, focused on cases involving African Americans, "other groups chose the educational arena as a battleground for community uplift and fought for their children's right to receive a quality education" (Williamson 2004, 112). Thus, in terms of both definitions of legalized segregation under state policies and the role of the decision on such policies, potential beneficiaries of the decision included Indians, Mexican Americans, Chinese Americans, and Japanese Americans.

The most frequently identified basis for the plaintiffs' case in *Brown v. Board of Education* is that of fairness and equity. However, at heart, the case was about access to educational opportunities and the impact of segregation on students (and, in turn, the need to desegregate schools). The specific premise underlying the plaintiffs' case was, in fact, twofold. First, the only way to ensure access to a quality education (which would certainly include access to educational resources) was for black and white students to be in schools together. Data indicated substantial inequities in funding across schools prior to and throughout the 1950s, such that "[s]chool expenditures were clearly not equal, as white schools were often funded at ten times the level of black schools in the same communities" (Waite 2004, 99). The Supreme Court's published opinion stated, "The plaintiffs contend that segregated public schools are not 'equal' and cannot be made 'equal,' and that hence they are deprived of the equal protection of the laws." As funding for K-12 education was controlled largely by local and state officials, a fair distribution of resources across black and white schools was unlikely. With regard to the implication that local and state officials were unlikely to change funding patterns, without Supreme Court or other federal intervention, the fact that the subsequent court decision was implemented slowly and with resistance in many places was reflective of how "external factors influenced the desegregation efforts of different communities and their opposition" (Williamson 2004, 111).

The second component of the premise in the plaintiffs' case was that the impact of segregation on students represented the basis for psychological damage that could be avoided or eliminated with desegregated schools. Among social scientists, segregation was defined as "restriction of opportunities for different types of associations between the members of one racial, religious, national or geographic origin, or linguistic group and those of other groups, which results from or is supported by the action of any official body or agency representing some branch of government" (Clark, Chein, and Cook 2004, 495). In the 1940s and early 1950s, a substantial body of research focused on the potential impact of segregation on students. The research results indicated that "segregation, prejudices and discrimination, and their social concomitants potentially damage the personality of all children—the children of the majority group in a somewhat different way than the more obviously damaged children of the minority group" (Ibid.). In this regard, the research showed that "as minority group children learn the inferior status to which they are assigned—as they observe the fact that they are almost always segregated and kept apart from others who are treated with more respect by the society as a whole—they often react with feelings of inferiority and a sense of personal humiliation" (Ibid., 495–496). While there is impact on the children's sense of self-worth and self-respect, the level of ambition and desire for educational attainment is affected, as well. And, while the evidence and impact of prejudicial behavior by individuals can be viewed as limited in meaning, if not necessarily isolated, that which is supported by the state was shown to have a far greater impact on the minority students.

In its instructions to the attorneys in *Brown*, the Court directed them to focus on "whether the framers of the Fourteenth Amendment [of 1868] had intended to act against school legislation" (Lieberman 1987, 310). Thurgood Marshall, lead counsel for the NAACP in this case, argued that "the historical record was unclear," in relation to prior civil rights legislation passed by the Congress in the 1800s and the *Plessy v. Ferguson* decision of 1896. And the Court agreed. Certainty concerning the framers' intentions was doubtful at best, not merely because of the difficulty in understanding the mindset of people seventy-five years before but also "'the status of public education at the time.' Public schooling in the 1860s was neither universal nor so vital as it was in 1954" (Ibid.).

Similarly, the difficulty in understanding the framers' intent (of the Constitution, as well as the early amendments and the Declaration of Independence) is evident in the complexity of their views regarding slavery and education. Constitutional scholar Richard Brookhiser notes that while a significant number of those who drafted the Declaration of Independence and the Constitution either owned or had previously owned slaves, most of them thought slavery was wrong. In the words of George Mason, a slave owner, "it brought 'the judgment of heaven on a country'" (Brookhiser 2006, 164). While others expressed similar concerns, they tended to be secular or pragmatic, rather than morally based, for the most part. In fact, "[s]ome founders feared that slaves would take reparations, or at least vengeance, through bloodshed" (Ibid., 165). Individuals, such as John Locke, equated the two concerns, suggesting "revolts against injustice were just" and that such a reaction "is not offence before God, but is that which he allows and countenances" (Ibid., 166). Thus, there was the sense that slavery was profitable, relatively unjust, and likely to end or be ended.

Whether the founders viewed all races as equal is not clear. Statements and actions of individuals, such as George Washington, Thomas Jefferson, Alexander Hamilton, and others, are both revealing of them and reflective of the time. Some statements cast Negroes as well as American Indians "variously as enemies to be feared, brutes to be scorned, children to be trained, natural men to be admired, or slaves to be worked" (Ibid., 170). Certainly, the issues of ability and pragmatism were at the center of the debates. Perhaps, Alexander Hamilton best encapsulated the founders' ultimate position: "Their natural faculties are probably as good as ours. . . . The contempt we have been taught to entertain for the blacks, makes us fancy many things that are founded neither in reason nor experience; and an unwillingness to part with property of so valuable a kind will furnish a thousand arguments against parting with it" (*Founders' Constitution* 2007). Thus, the two areas identified as "concrete instances of presumed equality of ability" and opportunities to evidence that ability were the "peacetime public responsibilities" associated with voting, for a limited historical period, and "fighting" in time of war (Brookhiser, 2006, 173). No matter the complexity and inconsistency of the founders' frame of reference, where education was concerned, the founders considered the principles that they articulated in relation to life, liberty, and the pursuit of either happiness or property (depending on which of the early documents is being considered) in this way: "These were statements of rights, not abilities. The founders were not saying that all men were equally talented or intelligent, nor did they care: as Jefferson put it, talents were 'no measure' of human rights" (Ibid., 170).

Where rights were concerned, "[t]he only compensation the founders contemplated for the decades of unpaid labor from which so many Americans had profited was education" (Ibid., 165). In particular, they encouraged both private and public education, worrying "less about who paid for education and who ran it than the end result: well-informed citizens who could sustain a republic" (Ibid., 130). Thus, the relationship between education and an informed citizenry capable of fully participating in society and contributing to its development was at the heart of the founders' understanding and ethos.

The Court's opinion in *Brown* sheds light on the lack of a clear legislative or constitutional intent regarding school legislation, as well as on the importance of access to education in 1954 and in future, indicating that

[i]n approaching this problem, we cannot turn the clock back to 1868, when the Amendment was adopted, or even to 1896, when *Plessy v. Ferguson* was written. We must consider public education in the light of its full development and its present place in American life throughout the Nation. Only in this way can it be determined if segregation in public schools deprives these plaintiffs of the equal protection of the laws. Today, education is perhaps the most important function of state and local governments. Compulsory school attendance laws and the great expenditures for education both demonstrate our recognition of the importance of education to our democratic society.

The Court addressed the importance of access to education directly in terms of decision making, career opportunities, and full "citizenship," including civic engagement—all aspects of full participation in society—noting:

It is required in the performance of our most basic public responsibilities, even service in the armed forces. It is the very foundation of good citizenship. Today it is a principal instrument in awakening the child to cultural values, in preparing him for later professional training, and in helping him to adjust normally to his environment. In these days, it is doubtful that any child may reasonably be expected to succeed in life if he is denied the opportunity of an education. Such an opportunity, where the state has undertaken to provide it, is a right which must be made available to all on equal terms.

The justices went on to address the issue of potential damage done to minority children with legalized segregation and the need to ensure an educational process and access to education not proscribed by race:

Does segregation of children in public schools solely on the basis of race, even though the physical facilities and other "tangible" factors may be equal, deprive the children of the minority group of equal educational opportunities? We believe that it does.

Here, influenced by the research associated with the psychological impact of segregation on African American children, they concluded:

The impact is greater when it has the sanction of the law, for the policy of separating the races is usually interpreted as denoting the inferiority of the negro group. A sense of inferiority affects the motivation of a child to learn. Segregation with the sanction of law, therefore, has a tendency to [retard] the educational and mental development of negro children and to deprive them of some of the benefits they would receive in a racial[ly] integrated school system. . . . Whatever may have been the extent of psychological knowledge at the time of *Plessy v. Ferguson*, this finding is amply supported by modern authority.

As indicated, the principle of access to education is not synonymous with access to desegregated education, from either a constitutional or a moral perspective. As constitutional scholar Jethro Lieberman puts it—given the focus during the first half of the twentieth century on education that was "separate but equal"—"[W]hy then insist on any schooling at all for the disfavored race? If schooling was a social, not a civil, right why bother even to debate? . . . If historical practice is the decisive factor, then the framers cannot be heard to have said even that separate black schools ought to be equal" (1987, 313).

The answer rests on at least two considerations: the presumption that access to education is necessary for all, in contribution to and participation in society; and, the realization that only education of quality and that which does not, in and of itself, inflict psychological harm fulfills the definition of education. Further, it is the responsibility of the state (i.e., the government and the law) to foster access to education that does not imply inferiority. Based on the Court's opinion, education can only achieve its goal if it does so.

The legal and political discussions of the impact of the *Brown* decision began shortly after the case was decided and have focused on the changing levels of segregation in schools (in general and in the North and the South), the role of the Supreme Court in making a statement for the country on a moral and policy-related issue, the limitations inherent in the decision (as it was issued, particularly in light of anticipated resistance), and analyses of subsequent court, legislative, and executive branch decisions related to discrimination.

To a large extent, many of the early discussions of the decision and its impact (and potential impact) focused on both the distinctiveness and importance of the case and less so on what changes had been realized.

In 1960, an article published in the *Modern Law Review* suggested that not only was the immediate impact of the case largely symbolic but that it "should not be judged by normal standards applied to court decisions" (Hartman 1960, 371). In this regard, it was suggested that compliance on the part of most states was based largely upon the fact that it was the judicial branch that had issued the ruling. Other than "a few states in the Deep South . . . throughout the rest of the country the prevailing attitude is one of respect for what the Supreme Court says is the law of the land" (Ibid., 371–372). And the sense of scholars and researchers was that the decision was consistent with "public opinion in a major part of the country—and, for that matter, world opinion" (Ibid., 371). The decision also reflected the idea that what was viewed as "the weakest of the three branches of government proved to be the only one with the conscience, the capacity, and the will to challenge the scandal, the immorality, the social and economic waste, and the positive dangers of racial discrimination" (Pritchett 1964, 869). Thus, discussions of the decision praised the Court "because it got the United States on the right side of history at a crucial time in world affairs." In this regard, the Court was described as having "made the right decision," forcing the country to address the issue of segregation. Subsequently, the executive and legislative branches "began to assume their responsibilities for achieving the broad purposes of racial equality. But if the Court had not taken that first giant step in 1954, does anyone think there would now be a Civil Rights Act of 1964?" (Ibid.).

The two major criticisms of the decision have related to the premise regarding the importance of integration in achieving equity and the extent to which the decision provided only broad guidelines for fulfilling the goals of educational access. Certainly, there have been those who have suggested that "*Brown* actually retarded the movement toward Black self-determination" (Howie 1973, 372), by focusing on the distractions of integration and assimilation. In this regard, some still question the very premise and value of integrated schools. Works such as "David Cecelski's 'Along Freedom Road' and Vanessa Siddle Walker's 'Their Highest Potential' argue the benefit of the segregated black school of the South for the children in those communities" (Waite 2004, 1999). Others question the motives of those who pursued desegregated education "as a yearning for assimilation and voluntary forfeiture of ethnic identity" (Williamson 2004, 111). While the analysis of the impact of the case twenty years after the decision re-flected a sense of "the decision's clarity about equality, . . . [it was noted that] confusion and conflict about equal education are prevalent. One reason has been growing controversy over whether racial equality requires desegregation. In 1954 the two seemed identical, but a few decades later integration no longer strikes many blacks as a requirement for equality" (Cohen 1974, 34). However, scholars in this area have addressed the challenge of avoiding "presentism, the unfortunate tendency to perceive the past solely through present-day lenses" (Dougherty 2004, 95), thus evaluating the motives and agenda of those who pursued the legal case fifty years earlier in light of the context of the twentieth or the twenty-first century.

Clearly, the suggestion that assimilation is the basis for ending segregation is controversial. However, from an academic standpoint, *Brown* offers students a unique opportunity "to think like historians, who do not uncritically accept simplistic or celebratory accounts of the civil rights movement" (Dougherty 2004, 95). Joy Ann Williamson of Stanford University concurs: "To teach Brown is to deconstruct simple notions of Civil Rights Movement triumphs and visions of a country eager to right historical wrongs" (2004, 109). She refers to the study of *Brown* as one of a number of attempts of "different groups (ethnic, gender, religious) . . . for educational access, quality, and equality [that] have influenced the nature of education for all American youth" (Ibid.).

While *Brown* has been lauded for its general statement of principle regarding access to education, it has been suggested that implementation of the decision met with resistance, largely because the Court did not establish clear guidelines for enforcement for the measurement of success. At the time of the ruling, many "southern officials had no intention of obeying the *Brown* ruling unless they were forced to do so. The decision played into the hands of southern officials because it was ambiguous to the point of not placing school districts under any real obligation" (Rodgers 1974–1975, 755). Thus, noncompliance was possible and not easy to address. According to political science scholar Harrell Rodgers, when the case was being argued, attorney "Thurgood Marshall asked the Court to establish specific deadlines for the start of school desegregation. Hindsight reveals that the Supreme Court made a serious mistake in ignoring Marshall's plea" (Ibid).

Thus, while *Brown v. Board of Education*, which was both ostensibly and in popular conception about segregation, is regarded as one of the pivotal legal decisions in U.S. history, how then can its impact be measured? Columbia University professor Cally Waite has indicated, "Students want to understand the significance of Brown because it is such a part of our popular historical culture, yet it is difficult to document the way in which Brown has changed schooling" (2004, 98). Waite has also said, "Did Brown really desegregate schools? This is . . . [a] valid question, but one that is problematic when one tries to reconcile the goals of the landmark case with the large number of segregated schools that exist today" (Ibid.). Thus, in many ways, *Brown* was viewed as a start in establishing the legal basis for school segregation but a tool of limited effectiveness on its own.

As the data indicate that school segregation did not end with the *Brown* decision or in the years following, to a large extent, why then is it considered a landmark case?

It appears that the significance of the case is linked to its impact more broadly, with regard to promoting access and defining a principle of equity. Certainly, many legal scholars, as well as scholars of history and education, agree that *Brown* was an important case symbolically and in reality. Also, the case has been identified as important in being chosen as the first case, preceding legal redress of other aspects of access to full participation in society, with subsequent legislation related to access to the political process, including the Voting Rights Act, and access to housing and employment.

In providing a summary of the legislation, case law, and executive orders that followed *Brown*, through the 1960s, Lieberman has noted the following:

The Civil Rights Act [Eisenhower] signed in 1957 was the first such law since the ill-fated Civil Rights Act of 1875. . . . [Subsequently, there was passage of] the 1964 Civil Rights Act, for the first time enforcing legislatively the Court's decision ten years earlier. That act declares unlawful all employment discrimination based on race, religion, creed, national origin, and sex, and bars discrimination in public accommodations and in any enterprise receiving federal funds. . . . Across a broad front during the 1960s, voting rights and other laws were put on the books, presidents issued executive orders, and the courts built a broad mosaic of equal protection doctrine. The Supreme Court led the way, striking down racial discrimination in area after area, finally reaching the most intimate relationship of all, marriage. In 1967, the Court unanimously voided miscegenation laws that prohibited blacks and whites from marrying. (1987, 315–316)

However, the *Brown* case only addressed the issue of legalized segregation. There are genuine "distinctions between *de jure* and *de facto* segregation: while southern schools were segregated by law, northern schools were segregated by circumstance. As a result, southern schools were ordered to desegregate, but northern schools were under no such edict immediately following Brown. . . . [and] if, according to the Supreme Court, segregated schools promoted a feeling of inferiority for children, must not that also be true in the North?" (Waite 2004, 99–100). Not surprisingly, in the absence of legalized segregation, similar types of separation occurred. Sometimes, segregation happened by chance, on the basis of socioeconomic factors and neighborhood choice, and sometimes by personal choice, such as the "alleged innate tendency of humans to associate with people of their kind, which was thought to be the basis of a 'natural' tendency towards segregation" (Hartung 2004, 89). Certainly, the other types of segregation did not have the force of law or the endorsement of the state. Thus, the legal decision and the subsequent legislation, and moves towards more equitable funding and educational opportunities were able to codify the broader principles related to fostering access to education and the philosophical statement regarding the importance of educational opportunities for the individual and for society. However, there were certainly limitations regarding the ability of case law and legislation to change other cultural and societal dynamics.

In light of the ongoing issue of segregation, *Brown* scholar Cally Waite has noted the importance of "the spirit and intent of Brown. . . . The victory went beyond abolishing segregated schooling and has been used as a template for a plethora of civil rights cases in the second half of the twentieth century" (Waite 2004, 99). As Waite has noted, in her teaching about the case, she chooses to "deliberately emphasize the spirit and intent of Brown, since it is difficult to ascertain the way(s) in which the decision has changed schooling" (Ibid.).

In the twenty-first century, the meaning of the *Brown* case continues to be discussed in light of current legal challenges, related to voucher programs in public schools (Viteritti 2002) and school desegregation programs, for example. In the 2007 case involving Seattle and Jefferson County, Kentucky, the Supreme Court ruled against the use of race in making public school assignments. In the case, "the court ruled unconstitutional the practice of 'racial balancing'" (Waldmeir 2007). As school segregation cases tend to hinge on the interpretation of the Constitution's establishment and equal protection clauses, the cases focus on the autonomy of school officials and the specific processes that are used to achieve racial balance in enrollments. Those writing the court's majority opinion and those in dissent in the Seattle case referred to the relationship to *Brown*, in terms of whether the intent of *Brown* had been realized and the true meaning of equality and fairness in society had been realized. While the 2007 decision may serve as the basis for precedent in other cases, Justice Roberts' opinion indicated that

Jefferson County's use of racial classifications has only a minimal effect on the assignment of students. Elementary school students are assigned to their first- or second-choice school 95 percent of the time, and transfers, which account for roughly 5 percent of assignments, are only denied 35 percent of the time—and presumably an even smaller percentage are denied on the basis of the racial guidelines, given that other factors may lead to a denial . . . Jefferson County estimates that the racial guidelines account for only 3 percent of assignments (Parents v. Seattle 2007).

While we do not suggest that greater use of race would be preferable, the minimal impact of the districts' racial classifications on school enrollment casts doubt on the necessity of using racial classifications (Ibid.).

The court's most recent decision in this area indicates that the future of the use of race in school assignments is in question. Justice Kennedy, who was a member of the majority in the ruling, "sided with the dissenters on one crucial point by stressing that school districts have 'a compelling interest . . . in avoiding racial isolation' of minority students and achieving 'a diverse student population.' He also complained that portions of the Roberts opinion 'imply an all-too-unyielding insistence that race cannot be a factor.' And he rejected the idea that the Constitution is unyieldingly 'colorblind'" (Ibid.).

Despite the arguments for and against segregation and the presumed bases for ongoing segregation, the *Brown* decision and subsequent rulings and discussions have focused on the goal of preparation for full participation in society. Thus, the key, overarching principle in the case and the constitutional intent, which informed the Court's 1954 decision, appears to be that of access—access to educational opportunities, in particular, and access to full participation in society, in a broader sense. *Opportunity for Leadership: Full and Informed Participation* addresses the need for access to education and access to information to ensure preparation for informed participation in society and informed decision making, supported by the premise articulated by the founders that an informed citizenry is the basis for a sound republic.

REFERENCES

"Alexander Hamilton to John Jay: 14 Mar. 1779." *The Founders' Constitution*, Volume 1, Chapter 15, Document 24. Chicago: The University of Chicago Press, 1987. Available at http://press-pubs.uchicago.edu/founders/documents/v1ch15s24.html (accessed January 31, 2008).

Brookhiser, Richard. *What Would The Founders Do?* New York: Basic Books, 2006.

Clark, Kenneth B., Isidor Chein, and Stuart W. Cook. "The Effects of Segregation and the Consequences of Desegregation: A (September 1952) Social Science Statement in the *Brown v. Board of Education of Topeka* Supreme Court Case." *American Psychologist* 59 (September 2004): 495–501.

Cohen, David K. "Segregation, Desegregation, and *Brown*: A Twenty-Year Retrospective." *Society* 12 (November/December 1974): 34–40.

Dougherty, Jack. "Teaching Brown: Reflections on Pedagogical Challenges and Opportunities." *History of Education Quarterly* 44 (Spring 2004): 95–97.

Hartman, Paul. "The United States Supreme Court and Desegregation: The Aftermath of *Brown v. Topeka*." *Modern Law Review* 23 (July 1960): 353–372.

Hartung, Uwe. "Research Into the Effects of Segregation and Its Role in *Brown vs. Board of Education*." *International Journal of Public Opinion Research* 16 (2004): 88–90.

Howie, Donald L. W. "The Image of Black People in *Brown v. Board of Education*." *Journal of Black Studies* 3 (March 1973): 371–384.

Lieberman, Jethro K. *The Enduring Constitution: A Bicentennial Perspective*. St. Paul, MN: West Publishing Company, 1987.

Parents v. Seattle School District No. 1 and Meredith v. Jefferson County Board of Education, 551 U. S. 05-908, 05-915 (2007) (Opinion of Roberts, C.J.). Available at http://www.supremecourtus.gov/opinions/06pdf/05-908.pdf (accessed February 4, 2008).

Pritchett, C. Herman. "Equal Protection and the Urban Majority." *American Political Science Review* 58 (December 1964): 869–875.

Rodgers, Harrell R., Jr. "The Supreme Court and School Desegregation: Twenty Years Later." *Political Science Quarterly* 89 (Winter 1974–1975): 751–776.

Viteritti, Joseph P. "Will the Supreme Court's Decision in Zelman End the Debate?" *Education Next* 2 (Summer 2002): 24–33.

Waite, Cally L. "The Challenge of Teaching Brown." *History of Education Quarterly* 44 (Spring 2004): 98–100.

Waldmeir, Patti. "Court Rules Out Schools' Racial Balancing." *The Financial Times* (June 28, 2007). Available at http://www.ft.com/cms/s/0/75039882-259b-11dc-b338-000b5df10621.html (accessed February 1, 2008).

Warren, C. J., Opinion of the Court. Supreme Court of the United States. 347 U.S. 483. *Brown v. Board of Education of Topeka.* Appeal from the United States District Court for the District of Kansas. Available at http://supct.law.cornell.edu/supct/html/historics/USSC_CR_0347_0483_ZO.html (accessed February 1, 2008).

Williamson, Joy Ann. "*Brown*, Black, and Yellow: Desegregation in a Multi-Ethnic Context." *History of Education Quarterly* 44 (Spring 2004): 109–112.

Wormser, Richard. "Gaines v. Canada (1938)." *Jim Crow Stories*, 2002. Available at http://www.pbs.org/wnet/jimcrow/stories_events_gaines.html (accessed September 19, 2006).

CHAPTER 2
The Value of Access to Information in a Competitive Environment

As we saw in the previous chapter, the value of access to education in support of full participation in society has been articulated by the framers of the Constitution and further clarified by the courts and scholars over time. So too have the issues of information and an informed citizenry, only less so. However, access to information is complicated by four interrelated factors: whether access to more information leads to better and more precise decision making; both the motives associated with and the impact of attempts to limit access to information; the fact that information is often available from a range of sources; and education is biased towards preparing individuals to locate and evaluate specific information (as opposed to making available a universe of all possible information).

The research has shown that access to information, when built upon prior educational preparation, makes individuals more competitive and better able to succeed in a range of circumstances, which in turn affords higher quality decision making in organizations. The research associated with the roles of those in highly responsible positions indicates that successful performance is tied to the gathering and use of information, from other individuals as well as print and electronic sources. A study published in the prestigious *Academy of Management Journal* found that when "competing theories of social capital" were compared, there was a positive correlation between career success, "assessed in terms of current salary, the number of promotions received over the entire career, and career satisfaction" and "access to information, access to resources, and career sponsorship" (Seibert, Kraimer, and Liden 2001, 219, 221). From an organizational perspective, the importance of effective information use is represented in the articulated concerns among employers that new graduates often lack much-needed analytical and critical thinking skills.

In terms of organizational leaders, an article entitled "The Synthesizing Leader," published in the *Harvard Business Review*, touts the ability to synthesize information as the key to establishing priorities (Gardner 2006). Management researcher and theorist Warren Bennis has discussed the need for leaders to use research and data in their work, indicating that leaders must allow themselves to know data and research (2004, 28–35; Michelman 2004). In the field of medicine, information is critical for leaders of medical teams faced with difficult and high-stakes decisions (Larson et al. 1998). And in engineering, the value of research has been noted because of the "important positive impact on economic performances." In collaborations between engineering firms and academic and other researchers, the application of research in the practical context has been discussed in terms of the value of "improving the economic relevance of scientific knowledge production" (Carayol 2003, 887).

In the context of information's importance to organizational leaders, the research has then focused not only on their access to information but also on their ability to evaluate information, in determining its quality and usefulness, and apply it in their decision making. In addition, information is also evaluated according to the specific context in which the organization finds itself and often in relation to specific and finite decision making circumstances. A significant body of literature associated with the issue of leadership competencies serves to identify the qualities and abilities possessed by successful leaders. Based on the study of leaders across a range of organizations, statements of leadership competencies can also be used as the basis for determining the types of educational and leadership training opportunities needed for future leaders (Barner 2000; Ulrich, Zenger, and Smallwood 2000). It does not appear to be coincidental that leadership competencies related to decision making and analytical skills have been identified as necessary for leaders in a range of professional contexts, or that access to information is a crucial component in developing these capabilities.

For young people, in particular, access to online information has become a necessary component of academic and professional preparation, as well as an effective means of leveling the playing field. Socioeconomic differences and biases based on race, ethnicity, and language have all been correlated with limited access to information. To this end, technology companies, particularly Apple Computer, which was the early leader in educational and academic computing through the late 1970s and the 1980s, and later Microsoft, IBM, and Dell established a long history of donating computers to schools and universities, with the added incentive of planting the seeds for future brand recognition. Ensuring that computers and Internet access are available, particularly given the smaller percentage of computers in homes in poor rural and urban communities, offers many schools (and public libraries) competitive advantages, as well. In addition, the focus on access to online information includes the opportunity to develop facility with computer and online searching and analytical skills: skills of market importance after graduation.

However, while the provision of access to technology, in general, and the Internet, in particular, has been identified as necessary in eliminating disparities, the research is inconclusive. While some findings indicate some potential benefit in academic development (Norman 1999), there are many more examples which indicate that the technology should be applied thoughtfully, rather than excessively, and in conjunction with effective instructional techniques. In other words, computer access in the classroom and the home does not guarantee that it will be put toward enhanced learning; as one researcher put it, "Too much computer exposure may hinder learning." The results of an international research study of "175,000, 15-year-old students in 31 countries" indicate that "if you overuse computers and trade them for other (types of) teaching, it actually harms the student" (MacDonald 2004).

In other words, access to information offers a competitive advantage to both the student and the school, but it cannot compensate for all possible effects of economic disparities. Similarly, more information, without sufficient academic preparation, is only part of the answer. At the same time, employers continue to emphasize the need for graduates who possess analytical and critical thinking skills. Simply opening the floodgates is clearly not enough and possibly too much of a good thing.

The amount of information available is often the focus of the discussion of access; and much has been written about information overload, both in terms of the expanding amount and types of information available and the increasing number of ways in which that information is made available. Yet, it is not only possible but also frighteningly easy to be "data-rich but information-poor" (Stueart and Moran 2002, 18).

Through attempts to increase access on one level, then, we come face to face with the irony of the more and the less. Nonetheless, there are just as many examples of concerted efforts to limit access, not based on amount of information, in responding to information overload, but that what is available is not suitable or appropriate for part or all of the population.

The number of recent and historical efforts to protect various segments of society by limiting access to information—from books and other publications to broadcast and entertainment media—is legion. Sometimes it takes the form of attempting to censor controversial statements of public figures in the media, by individuals and organizations on the left and the right of the political spectrum, including organizations never intended to be political (like the Federal Communications Commission), volunteer and grassroots groups, school boards, and publishers.

Some research suggests that young people who listen to music with sexually suggestive lyrics (Collins et al. 2004) or view television programs with provocative material (Martino et al. 2006) are more likely to engage in sexual behavior. The inevitable, potentially knee jerk reaction is to immediately limit access. However, it is important to note that of late the most vehement reactions have to do with violence or are not only sexual in nature. Often, both currently and historically, the information in question has a racial or cultural focus. *Huckleberry Finn* is a perennial favorite on censored reading lists, due to its use of the N-word. Other examples include the selection and labeling of textbooks, curricular decisions by school boards related to religious values (such as evolution), efforts to label music CDs, and limits on federal funding for libraries that do not install filtering software on their computers.

However, the more high-profile examples are related to the broadcast media, in particular that of the increased scrutiny and crackdown on the media by the FCC, circumstantially linked to Michael Powell's term as chairman (January 22, 2001–March 17, 2005) and subsequent to it. Two of the most highly publicized cases to date are an ABC network advertisement, which aired before *Monday Night Football* on November 15, 2004, and the 2004 Superbowl Halftime Show. Each incident involved African American and white protagonists; each received extensive press coverage and discussion in the media.

The commercial involved the Philadelphia Eagles' Terrell Owens and actress Nicollette Sheridan, who wore only a towel. *New York Times* writer William Rhoden describes the commercial: "In the introduction to the Monday night game between the Eagles and the Cowboys on ABC, Sheridan, who is white and stars in the ABC series 'Desperate Housewives,' asked Owens, who is black, to skip the game for her as they stood alone in a locker room. Sheridan dropped the towel—Owens's face lit up—and she jumped into his arms" (Rhoden 2004, 11). The reaction was swift, intense, and widespread. Tony Dungy, coach of the Indianapolis Colts, said, "I think it's stereotypical in looking at the players, and on the heels of the Kobe Bryant incident [in which Bryant was accused of sexual assault of a white woman]. I think it's very insensitive . . . [Dungy] was offended on three levels: as a member of the NFL, as a Christian, as an African-American" (Ibid.). Similarly, "Greg Aiello, an NFL spokesman, said . . . that Commissioner Paul Tagliabue was just as concerned and annoyed as Dungy" (Ibid.). Rhoden concludes that "Dungy was wise, and right to bring up the racial issue. A majority of NFL players are African-American. He knows the stereotypes, and he knows how hard it has been for African-Americans to become executives and coaches" (11). Rhoden also noted that he

wasn't offended that it depicted a white woman seducing a black man. White women and black men have been jumping into one another's arms for centuries—and folks have been up in arms about it for centuries. What . . . [he] found troubling was the reaction to the whole episode. It reflected a biased system that holds African-Americans to different standards of behavior. They are judged more harshly for the same offenses and given less credit for the same accomplishments. (Ibid.)

As Columnist Diane Roberts noted, "[t]he family values nation rose up, peppering ABC with complaints. They weren't offended that this low-rent seduction scene played into stereotypes about black men and white women. They just don't like nekkidness. Children could be watching!" (2004, 16A). As a result, "[t]he promo caught viewers by surprise, giving parents no time to keep children away from the set" (Ibid.).

Rhoden then moves on to the Jackson/Timberlake incident. Near the end of Janet Jackson and Justin Timberlake's musical performance during the 2004 Super Bowl halftime show, Timberlake pulled off an apparently breakaway part of Jackson's costume, revealing her breast. Rhoden indicated the following regarding the incident and the subsequent reaction:

He tore away a part of her costume and exposed her breast. Yet Timberlake was portrayed as the naïve white kid, and Jackson as the oversexed black temptress. Owens issued an apology Thursday; I haven't heard from Sheridan. A black woman has her clothes ripped off by a white man and she's demonized. A naked white woman jumps into a black man's arms, and he apologizes (11).

Another reporter described it this way: "[V]iewers gawked when Janet Jackson exposed one of her nipples during the Super Bowl halftime performance with Justin Timberlake," (Kennedy 2004) as if Jackson had masterminded the entire thing and tore away the fabric herself. Some months later, Timberlake acknowledged the difference in public response to Jackson and himself. As an interviewer noted, "In retrospect, Timberlake thinks he should have been held more responsible. 'I probably got 10 percent of the blame, and that says something about society,' he explains. 'I think that America's harsher on women. And I think that America is, you know, unfairly harsh on ethnic people'" (Moss).

Conversely, *New York Post* writer Phil Mushnick has suggested that the flack over the "cross-promo" of *Monday Night Football* and *Desperate Housewives* is not about race but about the tawdry nature of the commercial. Interestingly, he relates it to the Jackson/Timberlake situation, asking

Why on earth has race become even the slightest issue in this issue? Sheridan and Terrell Owens are pop figures and ABC threw them together. A nationally televised sports event was again chosen by its contracted network to serve as a desperate, sexually charged come-on. That was the issue. It was wrong in any and all colors. Mix 'em, match 'em, it was wrong. (2004, 67)

Both cases have also had an impact in terms of regulation and fines, with Mushnick noting that "the political power of Jackson's breast shows no sign of abating" (67). In this regard, the reactions and interpretations of reactions to the two incidents took place amid a backdrop of legislation and policy making, with increasingly harsh penalties for violators, and potentially as causes for such strong actions. For example, the House of Representatives passed a bill on March 11, 2004, whereby broadcasters would pay indecency fines of $500,000 per violation (up from $27,500). "Performers, under one provision of the House bill, would have been personally liable for up to $500,000 in fines" (Cave 2004, 946). At the same time, the Senate considered a similar law whereby broadcasters would have their licenses revoked after a third offense; it ultimately passed a measure called the Broadcast Decency Enforcement Act, which became law in June 2006 and increased the maximum fine for broadcasters tenfold to $325,000 per violation but did not include the fines for performers or the "three-strikes" provision.

For these and other reasons the Federal Communications Commission increased the scale of its enforcement, levying more than $1.7 million in fines between 2001 and 2004 (Cave 2004, 946). In the Super Bowl case alone, "the FCC fined CBS $550,000" (Kennedy 2004). However, the highest fine went to an episode of the CBS crime drama *Without a Trace*: $3.6 million, for portraying a teenage orgy scene (without nudity or a racial slant) in a character's flashback to a night of crime. This record surpassed the fines levied against Viacom, in relation to Howard Stern, that reached $3.3 million (Schatz 2006).

After the 2003 broadcast of the Golden Globe Awards, where singer Bono used a form of the F-word, the FCC established a policy "against accidentally aired profanities on TV and radio" (Neumeister 2007). The FCC determined that the ban was violated by a December 2002 Billboard Music Awards broadcast and a December 2003 Billboard awards show, in which performers used questionable language, although no fines were involved. "The FCC said the 'F-word' in any context 'inherently has a sexual connotation' and can be subject to enforcement action." However, in a June 2007, U.S. appellate decision, the court ruled that "some of the FCC's explanations for its new policy, reversing a more lenient policy in place for nearly three decades, were 'divorced from reality.'" In this regard, the U.S. Second Circuit Court of Appeals indicated that the use of potentially objectionable language is widespread and the policy was likely unconstitutional and returned the case to the Federal Communications Commission to let the agency try to explain how its policy was not "arbitrary and capricious" (Ibid.).

One result of the FCC's aggressive enforcement was a certain skittishness among media outlets. For example, "More than 60 ABC affiliates refused to air *Saving Private Ryan*, a highly acclaimed war movie that ABC was offering for Veterans Day [2004] broadcast. They feared the newly aggressive agency would impose fines for dirty language, not easily deleted from a film honored for depicting the harsh reality of men at war" (*USA Today* 2004, 10A). Many live broadcasts—such as the 2004 Academy Award ceremony on ABC, the Little League World Series on ESPN, and NASCAR broadcasts on NBC have been subject to 5-second delays (Carey 2004; Associated Press 2006; *Broadcast Engineering* 2004), while controversial scenes have been quickly deleted from videos and television programs. In an article entitled "The FCC's Full Frontal Assault on TV," (2006) writer John Eggerton refers to the FCC's "strict interpretation—however subjective—of the laws on the books" and expresses concerns about how the current climate is affecting cable and broadcast networks and the programming and content that is delivered. Thus, this climate of 'strict interpretation,' including its manifestation in more frequent penalties and higher fines, has led "writers and show creators . . . to chill their appetite for edgier fare" (18). It has been noted that, given the choice, broadcasters preferred "to self-censor rather than face the political storm." (Cave 2004, 946)

While there might be those who favor the censorship of material which they deem objectionable for themselves or for children, a climate that fosters self-censorship among broadcasters is of concern. The role of broadcasters in providing access to information, regarding a range of issues, from the advent and widespread use of television, and before, has been key to informing public opinion. The issue of more and less, with regard to access to information relates to the ability of the reader, viewer, or listener to evaluate the information critically, as opposed to limiting the information that is made available.

Members of both the left and the right have sought to censor statements made by media personalities. Immediately after 9/11, Falwell's comments clearly blame members of certain segments of U.S. society as the cause of terrorist attacks on U.S. soil. According to an interview with Falwell,

"God continues to lift the curtain and allow the enemies of America to give us probably what we deserve.... The ACLU [American Civil Liberties Union] has got to take a lot of blame for this," he said, charging that the rights organization is responsible for "throwing God out successfully, with the help of the federal court system, throwing God out of the public square, out of the schools.... The abortionists have got to bear some burden for this because God will not be mocked. And when we destroy 40 million little innocent babies, we make God mad. I really believe that the pagans and the abortionists and the feminists and the gays and the lesbians who are actively trying to make that an alternative lifestyle, the ACLU, People for the American Way [a Washington organization that opposes right-wing extremism]—all of them who have tried to secularize America. I point the finger in their face and say: 'You helped this happen.'"

On September 28, 2005, radio talk show host and former U.S. Secretary of Education Bill Bennett, in a discussion about abortion and social security pronounced, "[I]f you wanted to reduce crime, you could— if that were your sole purpose—you could abort every black baby in this country and your crime rate would go down" (CNN.com 2005). The Democrats, including Senate Minority Leader Harry Reid and House Minority Leader Nancy Pelosi, demanded an apology (Ibid.; Faler 2005). "Reid said he was 'appalled by Mr. Bennett's remarks and Mrs. Pelosi went on the House floor and demanded repudiations from congressional Republicans and President Bush, and an apology from Mr. Bennett. [She said that] 'Secretary Bennett's comments reflect a narrow-minded spirit that has no place within American discourse.'" (Pierce 2005, A11). A statement from the White House noted that Bennett's comments "were not appropriate" (Curl 2005, A03). U.S. Representative John Conyers, Jr., sent a letter, signed by a number of his colleagues, to the Salem Radio Network, which read,

It is difficult for us to understand how an individual granted a show on your network could utter such a statement in 21st century America. While we all support First Amendment Rights, we simply cannot countenance statements and shows that are replete with racism, stereotyping, and profiling.

Mr. Bennett's statement is insulting to all of us and has no place on the nation's public air waves. . . . We ask that you immediately suspend this radio program. . . . We are planning to convey our views to your commercial sponsors as well and hereby request a list of all sponsors of the show within the last year. (Buzzflash.com 2008)

U.S. Representative Melvin Watt, then chair of the Congressional Black Caucus, noted, "[I]t is obvious that these kinds of outrageous comments will continue unless there are economic consequences to those who make them. I, therefore, call on all radio station owners who carry Bill Bennett's show to immediately terminate the show and if they fail to do so, I call on his sponsors and advertisers to withdraw their advertising dollars" (Curl 2005, A03). Wade Henderson, executive director of the Leadership Conference on Civil Rights, expressed similar sentiments: "Bennett's statement is outrageous. As a former Secretary of Education, he should know better. . . . His show should be pulled from the air" (WashingtonPost.com 2005).

On the September 29 broadcast of his show, Bennett defended his statement as, essentially, thinking aloud and an attempt to explore ideas about abortion presented in the book *Freakonomics*. He "issued a statement about the furor," which read, in part, "A thought experiment about public policy, on national radio, should not have received the condemnations it has" (Curl 2005). Anger has continued at Bennett, but it appears that his career has not particularly suffered. In fact, Bennett was hired by CNN in early 2006 as a commentator, including his prominent role in CNN's November 2006 election night coverage, prompting some to suggest that the network "is more interested in posting sensational ratings than in putting thoughtful commentators on the air" (Hira 2006, 122).

While Howard Stern is perhaps the poster boy for media controversy, less frequently cited are comments made by radio personality Doug "The Greaseman" Tracht. On Martin Luther King Day, 1986, Tracht joked that if the assassination of one black man could result in an annual holiday, why not "kill four more and get the whole week off," for which he was suspended. Then, in 1999, on the day following the Grammy awards, he played a song by one of the winners Lauryn Hill, who is African American, and said to his listeners, "No wonder people drag them behind trucks." This statement came shortly after the dragging death of a black man in Texas. Public outrage was immediate: "This is the second time Tracht has had to apologize for failing to realize that Black lives are of consequence.... The Greaseman's comments are worse than racist, they lack the essential humanity that informs us that life has consequence. That mindset has no place in the media" (Williams 1999, 8). A similar response indicated, "Therein lies the difference between responsible talk radio and the racist charades that permeate much of the nation's airwaves." (Carter 1999, 10). A religious leader said, "I call upon all people of goodwill in America—Black and white, Jew and gentile, rich and poor—to denounce the Greaseman and ensure that he never, ever gets another chance to promote the killing of people just because of the color of their skin." The response from the management of the radio station, which went, "There is no room for remarks like that at our station and I apologize to all the listeners who were quite rightly offended by it" (Ahrens 1999, C01), resulted in Tracht's termination. It is important to note that Bill Bennett's program is still being broadcast (*Talkers Magazine* 2007). And, while there has been little coverage of Tracht since the 1999 incident, his show was back on the air on WMET, 1160 AM in the Washington, DC, metro area until November 2007.

And, on his April 4, 2007 broadcast, "in a phone conversation with his former sports correspondent Sid Rosenberg, [talk show host Don] Imus insults the Rutgers University women's basketball team. 'That's some nappy-headed hos,' he says" (Horn 2007, A21). Over the course of the next week, the comments were characterized using terms, such as "racist" or "unconscionable" by the NAACP, the National Association of Black Journalists (NABJ), and the presidents of Rutgers and the NCAA. On April 6, Imus apologized on his program, saying, "It was completely inappropriate, and we can understand why people were offended" (Ibid.). And "New York's WFAN-AM, Imus' flagship station" and CBS Radio also issued apologies. Calls for his firing came from NABJ President Bryan Monroe and the National Organization for Women, as well as other members of the media, including the *Today Show*'s Al Roker, *Daily News* columnist Filip Bondy, and *Philadelphia Inquirer* columnist Phil Sheridan, who wrote, "The First Amendment protects every American's right to freedom of speech. It doesn't protect racists' high-paying media jobs" (2007). Initially, Imus was given a two-week suspension by MSNBC and CBS Radio. Sponsors, including

Proctor & Gamble, Staples, Bigelow Teas, GM, and Sprint Nextel pulled their advertising from Imus' program. By April 12, MSNBC had announced the cancellation of the broadcast of Imus' program, and CBS announced that Imus had been fired.

Access to information and freedom of speech inform the very nature of democracy. While controversial statements can easily represent the worst sort of hatemongering, national dialogue on race and other issues is halted, when the focus is on silencing the offensive voices. They are clearly indefensible on the basis of accuracy, naivete, or positive intent. They, however, have led to both greater dialogue and enhanced scrutiny of policies and practices in organizations, which, if less provocative, did not always differ from those expressed by Bennett, Tracht, and others.

An example of a circumstance of gender with a racial undercurrent involved President Lawrence Summers of Harvard. In a 2005 speech to a scientific society, Summers addressed the underrepresentation of women and others in the sciences, in comments that he later described as an attempt to foster debate. Summers' reasons, purportedly based on research, were, most notoriously, life choices and innate cognitive differences between men and women, and not, as commonly believed, differences in socialization or discrimination (Kennicott 2005, C01). Furthermore, he claimed that research on the impact of socialization around male and female roles was disputed by his own experience: two toy trucks that he and his wife had given to his young daughters were quickly turned into the "mommy truck" and the "daddy truck," despite theirs being a household in which men and women were held to be equally competent. Strong reactions emerged from many quarters, including many Harvard faculty. Summers' comments followed other difficulties between himself and members of the faculty, including a highly publicized rift with African American studies scholar Cornel West. Eventually, with advising from a number of sources, including former president Bill Clinton, Summers announced his decision to commit $50 million to Harvard, in acknowledgement of the need to devote greater resources to the recruitment of women and minorities. When he eventually decided to step down as Harvard's president, he indicated that "the rifts between . . . [him] and segments of the arts and sciences faculty make it infeasible for . . . [him] to advance the agenda of renewal that . . . [he saw] as crucial to Harvard's future" (Braun and

Muskal 2006) admitting "there were moments when . . . [he] could have challenged the community more wisely and more respectfully" (Ibid.). Here, too, in the best light, Summers' controversial comments served to foster debate and challenge unspoken assumptions underlying his managerial philosophy and decision making.

Thus, while the controversial is often also the racial or the cultural, the provision of information about such circumstances serves both to inform the educational process and to ensure that efforts to influence the political and policymaking processes are informed by the current reality. Limiting access to information may not only suggest an overall inability to discern but also represent an attempt to provide access to only a proscribed set of ideas and viewpoints.

But what of the young? Clearly, the issues related to young people, access to information and their decision making are often the most controversial and relate to key decisions involving relationships and sexual activity. In Chapter 1, *Brown v. Board of Education* was identified as the first major case of the civil rights era, one that was both symbolic and effective, in codifying equity of access on the basis of the right of preparation for full participation in society. Since then, academic curricula and related textbook selection continue to be a battleground for promoting ideas of various types, in establishing policy and influencing students.

The current controversies related to K-12 curricula and textbook selection represent a special challenge to the principle of access to information, as "[p]ublic school textbooks' take on science, history, and sexuality can have tremendous influence on students. Religious groups usually have specific beliefs in these areas, and some are pushing to have their views reflected in public school teaching" (Religion Newswriters Association 2004). Thus, as a battleground for espousing views on various issues, conservative groups,

after repeatedly losing federal court battles on *constitutional grounds*, . . . have worked to get members elected to state and local school boards because courts have been reluctant to overturn decisions made by locally elected entities. . . . That's been coupled with the groups' efforts to present their views in a manner that can't be interpreted as promoting a specific religion. In response, civil liberties groups are more closely monitoring textbook battles and more willing to file lawsuits if they believe that any texts promote one faith group's beliefs over others—and thus violate the U.S. Constitution's establishment clause. (Ibid.)

In other words, while the decisions of individual school boards carry local or statewide influence, national and federal forces are not without impact. For example, a provision of the 1996 Personal Responsibility and Work Opportunities Reconciliation Act (more commonly known as "welfare reform" and later spelled out in Title V of the Social Security Act) "appropriat[ed] $250 million dollars over five years for state initiatives promoting sexual abstinence outside of marriage as the only acceptable standard of behavior for young people." In fact, "[f]rom 1998 to 2003, almost a half a billion dollars in state and federal funds were appropriated to support the Title V initiative" (Hauser 2004).

Thus, one of the challenges associated with abstinence-only education is the fact that while many of the curricular decisions in this regard are controlled by federal funding that limits the types of curricula that will be funded, the research related to abstinence-only education indicates that limiting access to information appears to have little positive impact with regard to sexual decisions or leads to poor decision making. Evaluations of abstinence-only education programs in a number of states, with regard to changes in behavior in the short term, have indicated that the programs have "had no impact on sexual behavior" in some cases, shown "increases in sexual behavior from pre- to posttest," or "mixed results" in other cases (Hauser 2004). In addition, "abstinence-only programs show little evidence of sustained (long-term) impact on attitudes and intentions. Worse, they show some negative impacts on youth's willingness to use contraception, including condoms, to prevent negative sexual health outcomes related to sexual intercourse" (Ibid.). The less-than-informed decision making appears to be based on a sense that the activities that constitute sex are few and that contraception and barrier protection are ineffective. Thus, if the goal is to keep young people from having sex, or to make responsible choices if they do have sex, abstinence-only education does not appear to accomplish these purposes.

At the same time, the textbook publishers wield considerable power, and adoption and purchase decisions by a few large states directly impact the rest of the country. Texas is one such state, and defined as a conservative one at that. For example, in 2004 the "Texas' State Board of Education adopted [several] new health textbooks that promote[d] traditional marriage and focus[ed] almost exclusively on abstinence among forms of birth control." As a result, "two messages" made crystal clear were: "abstinence should be taught without any textbook discussion of contraception," and "that the books should be explicit about marriage as a union between a man and a woman" (Teicher 2004, 12). These books were heavily supported by social and religious conservatives and opposed by many educators and public health advocates" (Religion Newswriters Association 2004). It appears that support for the change was led by State Board of Education member Terri Leo, a Republican from Spring, Texas, who was supported by nearly all of the other members. (Embry 2004, A1). The only member of the Board to oppose the change was Democrat Mavis Knight of Dallas, who voted against the new books because of the lack of information about contraception. Peggy Romberg, chief executive officer of the Women's Health and Family Planning Association of Texas, expressed similar concerns about not including information about contraception. And Randall Ellis, executive director of the Lesbian/Gay Rights Lobby of Texas, disapproved of the books because of the exclusive focus in defining marriage (Elliott 2004, B01).

Ironically, Texas has particularly high teenage pregnancy and birth rates. According to the Centers for Disease Control and Prevention's National Vital Statistics Report, at 62.6 live births per 1,000 female teenagers, aged fifteen to nineteen, Texas has the highest teenage birthrate of any U.S. state. While it is slightly lower than that of the District of Columbia and the same as that of Guam, the average for the nation is 41.1, such that Texas is roughly one and a half times the national average (Martin et al. 2006). Statistics related to teen pregnancy rates are somewhat less reliable, because pregnancies are not as easy to identify as births and are registered much less frequently and not typically compiled by the federal government as are vital birth statistics. However, of the most recent comprehensive statistics, Texas ranks fifth in terms of teen pregnancies, behind (in order) Nevada, Arizona, Mississippi, and New Mexico. And the state is twenty-sixth in terms of the abortion rate (Guttmacher Institute 2004). The issue of the state's high rate of teenage pregnancy might be viewed as a component of the relevance of the state as a center of the discussion of sex education and enhanced decision making, but it is also likely to fuel support on both sides of the debate related to abstinence-only education.

In addition to an overall "conservative market," Texas' adoptions are important, as it is one of only twenty-one states with a centralized process for reviewing textbooks (Teicher 2004, 12), such that the local decision making is not by town, city, or county but is statewide. One decision was made for all of Texas, influencing the entire U.S. market,

> because in the world of textbooks, as goes Texas—and, for that matter, California and Florida—so goes the rest of the nation. Texas, Florida and California combined make up 30 percent of the nation's $4 billion school textbook market. Textbook companies generally cut costs by marketing the same books chosen by these three states to the rest of the country. (Religion Newswriters Association 2004)

On the other hand, local mores and values are not without influence, as classroom and district level decisions often determine whether textbooks and curricula are in fact implemented. In Texas, at the time of the 2004 decision, state curriculum standards required students "to 'analyze the effectiveness and ineffectiveness of barrier protection and other contraceptive methods'" (Teicher 2004, 12), in effect inviting alternative points of view. Also, while the textbooks selected indicate the effectiveness of abstinence, "publishers will provide information on contraceptives in free supplemental materials—to give local school boards flexibility about whether to include those lessons in their curricula" (Ibid.).

While publishers are often criticized for shaping the market for the many by pandering to the few, they are also obliged to function in a marketplace that is varied, complex, and subject to scrutiny from many sides. The result is a "two-sided pressure [that] plays havoc with publishers, who try to respond to complaints of bias while attempting to write texts that meet the scattershot academic standards of different states" (Cavanagh 2005). Not surprisingly, pressure groups tend to focus their efforts in California and Texas. Those who argue against the state adoption process claim its demise would increase local control and curb the influence of outside lobbyists" (Ibid.). Others, such as Neal Frey of Educational Research Analysts, a conservative Christian textbook-reviewing organization, insist that "the current process ensures government accountability. Reverting to local control would result in textbook battles being fought eleven-hundred times in every school district around Texas" (Ibid.).

According to the Religion Newswriters Association, "[t]extbook battles waged by religious and social groups have been fought since the late 19th century." In the beginning, "Southern states organized to keep out textbooks that they saw as disparaging the Confederacy, so Northern publishers began sending separate books with more palatable references, like 'the War for Southern Independence'" (Teicher 2004, 12). Over time, the textbook battles intensified concerning the teaching of evolution, sex education, and history (Religion Newswriters Association 2004), of which none is more famous than the Scopes trial of 1925. Named after John Scopes, a Tennessee coach and substitute teacher who had essentially volunteered to be the defendant, it quickly became a test case against the recently passed Butler Act, which forbade the teaching of evolution in state-funded schools.

In many ways, it is not surprising that textbook selection and curricular decisions have been the battlegrounds for such key cultural issues, given the symbolic and economic impact of such decisions. Even in the age of electronic access to information on many subjects and from many sources, "students spend somewhere between 50 percent and 90 percent of class and homework time focused on textbooks" (Teicher 2004, 12). Thus, what is emphasized in a textbook and reinforced in the classroom is likely to have a tremendous impact on students in their access to information and their decision making.

The issue of school board decisions regarding curricula and textbook selection leads directly to the issue of suppressing comments made by prominent individuals on educational matters. In November 2005, following a decision by the school board of Dover, Pennsylvania, related to intelligent design, Pat Robertson made the following statement on his television program, "The 700 Club":

I'd like to say to the good citizens of Dover: if there is a disaster in your area, don't turn to God, you just rejected him from your city.... And don't wonder why he hasn't helped you when problems begin, if they begin. I'm not saying they will, but if they do, just remember, you just voted God out of your city. And if that's the case, don't ask for his help because he might not be there. (Zeliger 2005)

Often thrusting unsuspecting local school boards under a national spotlight, in such a way, decisions regarding access to information, whether in K-12 education or in the media, become the focus of substantial societal attention and debate.

Finally, recent legislation reflects our conflicting societal principles related to access to information. In the post-9/11 period and the ongoing war on terror, both the original USA Patriot Act and the reauthorized version brought to the foreground competing principles of access to information and privacy. With increased access to phone, cell phone, and e-mail records, public opinion polls reveal a willingness among the majority of people to sacrifice some personal privacy in favor of enhanced security. Similarly, the Sarbanes-Oxley Act was signed into law in order to address cases of corporate fraud and to hold organizational leaders personally accountable for the inaccuracy of financial reporting. In each case, claims Berlau (2006), "it was rushed through after a crisis, and many provisions weren't scrutinized." While provisions in the original Patriot Act related to privacy have been challenged and, in some instances, revised in the 2006 version, Sarbanes-Oxley has been used as the basis for enhanced power and latitude by agencies such as the Department of Justice, including the U.S. Attorney General. Sarbanes-Oxley has made organizational leaders and members of boards of directors potentially liable for not providing access to information requested by investigatory agencies. In this context, law enforcement agencies have indicated a willingness to push the boundaries of the law in their investigations, possibly sacrificing privacy and other perceived constitutional protections associated with privacy to see justice done. Such was the case with the prosecutor in the Valerie Plame/ *Time* magazine leak investigation, who pressured the management and the board of *Time* to turn over the reporter's notes, threatening their own financial assets, as well as in the FBI search of U.S. Representative William Jefferson's office. Both represented unprecedented uses of power by federal investigative and law enforcement agencies, which exerted authority under new laws or in the general climate of empowerment of investigative and law enforcement or prosecutorial agencies, in seeking justice.

In the post-Enron and post-9/11 era, with legislation such as Sarbanes-Oxley that reflects an emphasis on openness, access to information, accuracy of information over protection of individual or organizational privacy, the nature of access to information as a societal principle remains as controversial as ever.

REFERENCES

"A Racy TV Promo Gets Iced, and So Does 'Private Ryan'." *USA Today* (November 19, 2004): 10A.

Ahrens, Frank. "Congress Agrees to Raise Broadcast-Indecency Fines." *The Washington Post* (May 20, 2006): D01. Available at http://www.washingtonpost.com/wp-dyn/content/article/2006/05/19/AR2006051901611.html (accessed September 18, 2006).

————. "'Greaseman' Suspended for Racist Remark; WARW Pulls Doug Tracht Off the Air, Offers Apology." *The Washington Post* (February 25, 1999): C01.

Barner, Robert. "Five Steps to Leadership Competencies." *Training and Development*, 54 (March 2000): 47–52.

"Bennett Under Fire for Remarks on Blacks, Crime." CNN.com (September 30, 2005). Available at http://www.cnn.com/2005/POLITICS/09/30/bennett.comments/ (accessed April 14, 2006).

Bennis, Warren. "The Seven Ages of the Leader." *Harvard Business Review* 82 (January 2004): 28–35.

Berlau, John. "Sarbanes-Oxley vs. the Free Press." *Reason* 37 (January 2006): 48–51.

Braun, Stephen, and Michael Muskal. "End of Summers Days at Harvard." *Chicago Tribune* (February 22, 2006). Available at http://docs.newsbank.com/openurl?ctx_ver=z39.88-2004&rft_id=info:sid/iw.newsbank.com:NewsBank:CTRB&rft_val_format=info:ofi/fmt:kev:mtx:ctx&rft_dat=10FF12A63A549E00&svc_dat=InfoWeb:aggregated5&req_dat=0FF0DDC272369ADF (accessed January 30, 2008).

Buzzflash.com. "Conyers Calls on Network to Suspend Bill Bennett's Radio Program." *Buzzflash.com* (September 29, 2008). Available at http://www.buzzflash.com/alerts/05/09/ale05151.html (accessed January 31, 2008).

Carayol, Nicholas. "Objectives, Agreements and Matching in Science-Industry Collaborations: Reassembling the Pieces of the Puzzle." *Research Policy* 32 (June 2003): 887–908.

Carey, Matt. "ABC to Impose Delay on Oscar Telecast." CNN.com (February 5, 2004). Available at http://www.cnn.com/2004/SHOWBIZ/Movies/02/05/sprj.aa04.abc.oscar.delay/index.html (accessed January 30, 2008).

Carter, Richard. "Some Radio Talk-Show Hosts Talk Too Much." *The New York Amsterdam News* 90 (15) (April 8, 1999): 10. Available at http://search.ebscohost.com/login.aspx?direct=true&db=aph&AN=1670516&site=ehost-live (accessed January 31, 2008).

Cavanagh, Sean. "Reading From the Right." *Education Week* 25(4) (September 21, 2005). Available from Academic Search Premier, http://search.ebscohost.com/login.aspx?direct=true&db=aph&AN=18414349&site=ehost-live (accessed January 31, 2008).

Cave, Damien. "Decency Battle Rages On." *Rolling Stone* 946 (April 15, 2004): 44.

Collins, Rebecca L., Marc N. Elliott, Sandra H. Berry, David E. Kanouse, Dale Kunkel, Sarah B. Hunter, and Angela Miu. "Watching Sex on Television Predicts *Adolescentiation* of Sexual Behavior." *Pediatrics* 114(3) (September 2004): e280–e289. Available at http://pediatrics.aappublications.org/cgi/reprint/114/3/e280?maxtoshow=&HITS=10&hits=10&RESULTFORMAT=&fulltext=Watching+Sex+on+Television+Predicts+Adolescent&andorexactfulltext=and&searchid=1&FIRSTINDEX=0&sortspec=relevance&resourcetype=HWCIT (accessed January 31, 2008).

Curl, Joseph. "Bennett's Remarks 'Inappropriate.'" *The Washington Times* (October 1, 2005): A03.

Dionne, E. J., Jr. "Talk, Talk, Talk. We'd Rather Yap about Imus than Deal with the Real Problems." *Pittsburgh Post-Gazette* (April 17, 2007): B7.

Eggerton, John. "The FCC's Full Frontal Assault on TV." *Broadcasting & Cable* 136 (March 20, 2006): 1–19.

Elliott, Janet. "Altered School Books Given Board Approval; Texts Rewritten to Define Marriage as Between a Man and a Woman." *Houston Chronicle* (November 6, 2004): B01.

Embry, Jason. "Textbook Approval Hits Bump; State Board Member Wants Texts to Clarify Marriage, Condemn Homosexuality." *Austin American-Statesman* (November 5, 2004): A1.

Faler, Brian. "Bennett Under Fire for Remark on Crime and Black Abortions." *The Washington Post* (September 30, 2005): A05.

Gardner, Howard. "The Synthesizing Leader." *Harvard Business Review* 84 (February 2006): 36–37.

Hauser, Deborah. "Five Years of Abstinence-Only-Until-Marriage Education: Assessing the Impact." advocatesforyouth.org (2004). Available at http://www.advocatesforyouth.org/publications/state evaluations/index.htm (accessed September 30, 2006).

Hira, Nadira A. "Shock Jock." *Essence* 36 (April 2006): 122.

Horn, J. "The Imus Scandal: Chronology and Aftermath." *Los Angeles Times* (April 13, 2007): A21.

Kennedy, Sarah. "Outrage Nothing New in Pop Culture: Shock to the System." calgarysun.com (October 21, 2004). Available at http://www.calgarysun.com/cgi-bin/publish.cgi?p=89343&x= articles&s=showbiz (accessed October 1, 2006).

Kennicott, Philip. "The Man in The Ivory Tower." *The Washington Post* (April 15, 2005): C01.

Larson, Jr., James R., Caryn Christensen, Timothy M. Franz, and Ann S. Abbott. "Diagnosing Groups: The Pooling, Management, and Impact of Shared and Unshared Case Information in Team-Based Medical Decision Making." *Journal of Personality and Social Psychology* 75 (July 1998): 93–108.

"Little Leaguer Cusses, Manager Hits Him." MSNBC.com (August 22, 2006). Available at http://www.msnbc.msn.com/id/14466871/ (accessed January 30, 2008).

MacDonald, G. Jeffrey. "Contrarian finding: Computers Are a Drag on learning." *The Christian Science Monitor* (December 6, 2004). Available at http://www.csmonitor.com/2004/1206/p11s01-legn.html (accessed October 9, 2006).

Martin, Joyce A., Brady E. Hamilton, Paul D. Sutton, Stephanie J. Ventura, Fay Menacker, and Sharon Kirmeyer. "Births: Final Data for 2004." *National Vital Statistics Reports* 55 (September 2006). Available at http://www.cdc.gov/nchs/data/nvsr/nvsr55/nvsr55_01.pdf (accessed March 19, 2007).

Martino, Steven C., Rebecca L. Collins, Marc N. Elliott, Amy Strachman, David E. Kanouse, and Sandra H. Berry. "Exposure to Degrading Versus Nondegrading MusicLyrics and Sexual Behavior Among Youth." *Pediatrics* 118(2) (August 2006): e430–e441. Available at http://pediatrics.aappublications.org/cgi/reprint/118/2/e430?maxto show=&HITS=10&hits=10&RESULTFORMAT=&fulltext=Expo sure+to+Degrading+Versus+Nondegrading+Music&andorexactfull text=and&searchid=1&FIRSTINDEX=0&sortspec=relevance& resourcetype=HWCIT (accessed January 31, 2008).

Michelman, Paul. "What Leaders Allow Themselves to Know." *Harvard Management Update* 9 (February 2004): 3–5.

"Morality and the Broadcast Media: A Constitutional Analysis of FCC Regulatory Standards." *Harvard Law Review* 84 (January 1971): 664–699.

Moss, Corey. "Justin's Future Shock." MTVnews.com. Available at http://www.mtv.com/bands/t/timberlake_justin/news_feature_081506/ (accessed February 12, 2007).

Mushnick, Phil. "Racy Doesn't Mean Racial. Don't Make MNF's Towel Stunt a Black and White Issue." *The New York Post* (November 21, 2004): 67.

"NBC Sports Introduces Delay into NASCAR Racing Coverage." *Broadcast Engineering* (October 14, 2004). Available at http://broadcastengineering.com/newsrooms/nbc-nascar-delay-20041015/ (accessed January 30, 2008).

Neumeister, Larry. "Broadcasters Win FCC Expletive Dispute." FoxNews.com (June 5, 2007). Available at http://www.fox news.com/wires/2007Jun05/0,4670,BroadcastIndecency,00.html (accessed January 30, 2008).

Norman, Jessy. "Negative Effects of Computers in Classrooms." USAToday.com (December 13, 1999). Available at http://courses.wcupa.edu/fletcher/english121/projects/10b/jessy.htm. (accessed January 30, 2008).

Pierce, Greg. "Nation Inside Politics." *The Washington Times* (September 30, 2005): A11. Available at http://docs.newsbank.com.libproxy.lib.unc.edu/openurl?ctx_ver=z39.88-2004&rft_id=info:sid/iw.newsbank.com:NewsBank:WSTB&rft_val_format=info:ofi/fmt:kev:mtx:ctx&rft_dat=10CF60CB2BCD16C8&svc_dat=InfoWeb:aggregated5&req_dat=0FF0DDC272369ADF (accessed January 31, 2008).

Rhoden, William C. "In 'Monday Night' Fallout, A Deeper Racial Issue." *The New York Times* (November 21, 2004): 11.

Roberts, Diane. "Don't Get Your Knickers Twisted: Morality Isn't Just about Sex." *The St. Petersburg Times* (December 18, 2004): 16A.

Roberts, Selena. "Ignorance and Arrogance Collide, Live and Off Color." *The New York Times* (June 10, 2004): D1.

Saunders, Doug. "U.S. Got What It Deserves, Falwell Says." *The Globe and Mail* (September 15, 2001): A2.

Schatz, Amy. "FCC Levies Record Indecency Fine on CBS Show." *The Wall Street Journal* (March 16, 2006). Available http://online. wsj.com/public/article/SB114245387453999194-v0XjLy5pPdmcNb HiFO_DWw3aYX0_20070315.html?mod= (accessed September 18, 2006).

Seibert, Scott E., Maria L. Kraimer, and Robert C. Liden. "A Social Capital Theory of Career Success." *Academy of Management Journal* 44 (April 2001): 219–237.

Sheridan, Phil. "When Hate Meets Ignorance on the Air." *The Philadelphia Inquirer* (April 7, 2007). Available at http://docs.newsbank.com/ openurl?ctx_ver=z39.88-2004&rft_id=info:sid/iw.newsbank.com: NewsBank:PHIB&rft_val_format=info:ofi/fmt:kev:mtx:ctx&rft_dat= 118C0908730A6418&svc_dat=InfoWeb:aggregated5&req_dat= 0FF0DDC272369ADF (accessed January 30, 2008).

Stueart, Robert D., and Barbara B. Moran. *Library and Information Center Management*. Sixth edition. Greenwood Village, CO: Libraries Unlimited. 2002.

Teicher, Stacy A. "In Texas, a Stand to Teach 'Abstinence Only' in Sex Ed." *The Christian Science Monitor* (November 9, 2004): 12.

"Texas Textbook Vote Has National Implications." Religion Newswriters Association (November 8, 2004). Available at http:// www.religionlink.org/tip_041025b.php (accessed April 4, 2006).

"The Top Talk Radio Audiences." *Talkers Magazine* (February 2007). Available at http://www.talkers.com/main/index.php?option=com_content&task=view&id=17&Itemid=34 (accessed January 31, 2008).

Williams, Armstrong. "Rock Newman Attempts to Orchestrate the Deejay Greaseman's Attonement." *The New York Amsterdam News* 90 (11) (March 11, 1999): 8. Available at http://search.ebscohost.com/login.aspx?direct=true&db=aph&AN=1670486&site=ehost-live (accessed January 31, 2008).

Ulrich, Dave, Zenger, Jack, and Norm Smallwood. "The New Leadership Development." *Training & Development* 54 (March 2000): 22–27.

"U.S. Teenage Pregnancy Statistics: Overall Trends, Trends by Race and Ethnicity." New York: Guttmacher Institute, 2004. Available at http://www.guttmacher.org/pubs/2006/09/12/USTPstats.pdf (accessed January 30, 2008).

Yang, Catherine, and Richard S. Dunham. "Oh Janet, What Hast Thou Wrought?" *BusinessWeek* 3875 (March 22, 2004): 59.

Zeliger, Robert. "Dover Raps Roberston, Clings to Intelligent Design." *The Village Voice* (November 14, 2005). Available at http://www.villagevoice.com/news/0546,zeliger,70015,2.html (accessed January 30, 2008).

CHAPTER 3
The Controversy over Access to Information

As we have seen, controversies over access to information are related to whether access to more information leads to better and more precise decision making. Similarly, the challenge of full participation by a given individual is directly affected by the complexity of the many issues about which people need to be fully informed. In the case of decision making associated with major and controversial societal issues, the complexity of the issues, as supported by access to more information, is reflected in the difficulty associated with decision making by the many—that is, public opinion—and the interpretation of those decisions. The discussion of access to information provides a basis for the analysis of decision making in the aggregate, as measured by public opinion polls. While the public does not necessarily make decisions regarding the establishment or interpretation of public policy, it does have opportunities to influence that policy, by its voting decisions and via statements of opinion, which are acknowledged to inform the legislative, policymaking, and judicial processes, as will be discussed in greater detail.

The published research reflects the fact that more information, as measured by the amount and expansion of available content, influences decision making but in ways that are quite complex. In the case of two of the more controversial societal issues—abortion and the death penalty—discussion is not only indicative of their controversial nature but also reflective of ongoing analyses of public opinion—decision making—over time, despite (or perhaps because of) changes in the amount and types of information available.

In the case of the death penalty, Cochran and Chamlin (2005) note that "public opinion polling prior to the [1972] Furman [*v. Georgia*] decision was quite crude and simplistic and had undergone very little scrutiny" (574). However, Supreme Court Justice Thurgood Marshall has been credited with challenging this early research and noting the importance of public opinion in decisions of the Court. In the landmark Furman decision, he

emphasized the importance of public opinion as a direct indicator of the "evolving standards of decency" necessary to assess the constitutionality of capital punishment under the Eighth Amendment. Marshall noted that a punishment was invalid if "popular sentiment abhors it" and that "it is imperative for constitutional purposes to attempt to discern the probable opinion of an informed electorate." (Ibid.)

Since then, the courts, particularly the Supreme Court, have acknowledged the importance of, not only constitutionality but also "prevailing public standards" in their rulings.

Since 1972, the level and types of available information associated with capital punishment have expanded dramatically, due, in large part, to the increased availability of information regarding forensics and DNA evidence in the news media. Discussions of DNA evidence (including relatively widespread disclosure of the processes and fallibility of analyses of such evidence and instances of mistakes made by those collecting such evidence and laboratories in evaluating it), the overturning of older death penalty cases and other convictions, and the determination that executed individuals were later cleared or at least not linked to victims using DNA evidence have made it that much more difficult for individuals and society to develop clear-cut opinions regarding the rightness or wrongness of the death penalty. In particular, DNA was featured in the widely publicized case of the questionable confession of John Mark Karr, when there was not a match with the evidence found at the scene of the death of Jon Benet Ramsey. In addition, a sociocultural and socioeconomic dimension has come to light regarding sentencing, in general, and the death penalty, in particular, with research related to the extent to which the death penalty is applied more frequently in the cases of poor and minority inmates, as well as the controversy over harsher sentencing guidelines for crack cocaine, which has more minority users, as compared with powder cocaine, which has more white users. In particular, the research indicates that in death penalty cases, black-on-white crime led to the highest percentage of death sentences, followed by black-on-black crime, followed by crime by any nonblack defendant regardless of the race of the victim (Baldus et al. 1998, 1638–1770). With regard to the sentencing differences with cocaine, "the federal government makes a great distinction between powder cocaine, usually snorted, and crack cocaine . . . which is smoked. According to federal law, a person who is caught in possession of five grams of crack gets an automatic mandatory minimum sentence of five years in prison. . . . Possessing cocaine in its powder form does not carry a mandatory minimum" (Sabet 2005, 182).

Until relatively recently, once cases had been decided and the death penalty imposed, much of the subsequent process was unseen by the general public. The sole exceptions were appeals in court, public statements by attorneys and families of or other spokespersons for the victims or the convicted, governors' decisions regarding granting stays of execution, and reporters' and prison officials' statements of the details related to last meals and last words. However, far more information about individual death penalty cases is now made available in the news and popular media. Not surprisingly, in the early 2000s "numerous public opinion polls taken over the past several years indicated the lowest recorded level of death penalty support since the mid-1960s and the greatest drop in support ever recorded" (Bohm 2003, 191–192; Cochran and Chamlin 2005, 575).

The role of forensics and DNA evidence in real-world cases has come to public consciousness, through a set of highly popular television programs, such as *Crime Scene Investigation*, that focus on forensic investigations of crime scenes. The widespread sense that justice relies on forensics evidence and that such evidence is consistently reliable has resulted in what is known as the "CSI effect": an increased willingness on the part of juries to believe forensics evidence over testimony (Tyler 2006). Of death penalty cases, most are murder cases. However, DNA evidence transcends cases of murder, to include those involving sexual assault, the most highly publicized of which, involving the

Duke University lacrosse team rape investigation, also has a social element.

The "CSI effect" is documented by both the perceptions of trial lawyers and legal scholars and research in related aspects of juror behavior. While the phenomenon is too new to be the subject of extensive empirical research, NYU law and psychology professor Tom Tyler believes that

[t]he CSI effect has become an accepted reality by virtue of its repeated invocation by media. Although no existing empirical research shows that it actually occurs, on a basic level it accords with the intuitions of participants in the trial process. The suggestion that watching CSI might raise juror standards is consistent with empirical findings in other areas of legal psychology. There are large research literatures in the field supporting the argument that the mass media presentation of crime could produce a CSI effect of some kind. (2006)

The CSI effect attests to how increased availability of information complicates both the decision making process and interpretation of those decisions. Tyler claims,

It is equally plausible, however, that CSI might have an effect opposite of that which has been suggested. CSI might aid the prosecution in lowering juror standards. The psychological literature on reactions to crime demonstrates that people want to see justice for victims. In the aid of this desire, standards for evidentiary sufficiency waver. The emotional desire to punish the criminal and restore moral balance of the community can overwhelm the cognitive search for truth.

In this regard, "[w]hen jurors are motivated to identify and punish a wrongdoer, they can exaggerate the value of scientific evidence, viewing it as overly conclusive" (Ibid.). In other words, whether the focus is ensuring that justice is done for the accused or the victim—or making the case for the prosecutor or the defense—forensics evidence plays a much more prominent role in jury decisions today than it did in the past.

Capital punishment, too, has received greater exposure through such movies as *Dead Man Walking* and *The Green Mile*, both likely influenced by the earlier and well-known book and movie *In Cold Blood*. While these depictions detailed the psychological and other preparations of the convicted, they also presented, for example, information about the administering of the lethal injection or gas or electric current and the body's physiological response to them. Thus, the exposure and analysis of such details may serve to display what some might view as the barbarism of the execution. Add the disclosure of the convicted felon's background, family members, articulated rationale for the crime, and pleas of innocence and/or for leniency, among other things, and the circumstances of the crime take second place to the criminal's sudden humanization. Television programs like *Oz*, reality programs such as *Court TV*, and the increased use of cameras in the courtroom also provide "inside access" to real and fictionalized criminal and civil cases and prison life.

Justice Thurgood Marshall addressed the issue of how information's value and reliability affect public opinion, noting "that the probative value of public sentiment regarding capital punishment was limited only to an informed and knowledgeable opinion" (Cochran and Chamlin 2005, 574). Drawn from his opinion on *Furman v. Georgia*, the so-called "Marshall hypotheses"

spawned a considerable body of empirical testing. The three Marshall hypotheses are: (1) support for capital punishment is inversely associated with knowledge about it, (2) exposure to information about capital punishment produces sentiments in opposition to capital punishment, but (3) exposure to information about capital punishment will have no impact on those who support it for retributive reasons. (Ibid., 573)

The results of the studies have "tended to find somewhat mixed though relatively consistent support for the three Marshall hypotheses. That is, informed opinion is less supportive of capital punishment; exposure to information tended to reduce support for capital punishment; and retributivists tended to be immune to the effects of information about capital punishment" (Ibid., 574).

In an article further addressing the question of whether information can change public opinion regarding the death penalty, Cochran and Chamlin found that these tests, by and large, supported Marshall's hypotheses, specifically:

(1) exposure to information might polarize opinion, (2) death penalty sentiments which had been publicly pronounced were more resistant to change,

(3) initial beliefs about the death penalty such as its general deterrent effect or marginal incapacitation effect were not changed by information of these issues, (4) when attitudes toward capital punishment changed, the change was primarily due to information regarding racial disparities in justice and/or the execution of innocent persons, and finally (5) changed death penalty opinions tended to rebound to their original, preinformed positions. (Bohm 1998, 40–41; Bohm 2003, 43–44; Cochran and Chamlin 2005, 574)

They also noted that: prosecutors sought the death penalty more frequently, if supported by public opinion; "trial judges might feel pressured to impose death sentences even when it might not be appropriate and appellate judges might feel pressured to uphold these sentences due to their perceptions of strong public support;" and "governors might be more inclined to support death penalty legislation and sign execution warrants and less inclined to consider commutations and pardons for death row inmates if they perceived strong public support for capital punishment" (2005, 573).

Dissecting the process of criminal investigation, disclosing the intricacies and limitations of the use of scientific evidence, presenting data regarding presumed societal inequities in applying the death penalty, humanizing the convict, and revealing the details of the execution represent more than the provision of access to more information for the general public. This increase in information also serves to make the decision making more abstract, personal, and uncomfortable. As jury members embrace the most scientific of the information presented to them, so does public opinion overall seek to retain the option of correcting a wrong decision. Thus, at least where DNA and forensics evidence are concerned, more information does not necessarily lead to better, more informed decisions.

Like the death penalty, the issue of abortion is extremely controversial. While the topic of abortion has continued to be a subject of intense debate since the 1973 *Roe v. Wade* decision, the increased information appears to be reflected in the nature of public opinion—not necessarily changing but intensifying and complicating the decision making process and its interpretation.

According to public opinion expert Karlyn Bowman, the public is "[r]ock solid in its absolutely contradictory opinions" where abortion is concerned. In this regard, "[a] solid majority long have felt that Roe v.

Wade should be upheld. Yet most support at least some restrictions on when abortions can be performed. Most think having an abortion should be a personal choice. But they also think it is murder" (Benac 2006). A recent poll by AP-Ipsos found that "most Americans are ensconced in what one policy analyst calls the 'big mushy middle' on this issue. . . . 19 percent of Americans said abortion should be legal in all cases; 16 percent said it should never be legal; 6 percent did not know. That left nearly three-fifths somewhere in between, believing abortion should be legal only under certain circumstances" (Ibid.).

Roe v. Wade is typically lauded as a case that focuses on choice in a free society. However, the 1973 decision hinged on the issue of privacy. While the word privacy does not appear in the Constitution or in the Bill of Rights, various amendments have been interpreted to preserve rights of privacy, related to one's home (First Amendment), freedom from illegal search and seizure (Fourth Amendment), and avoiding self-incrimination (Fifth Amendment). In *Roe v. Wade*, the Supreme Court ruled that the right to privacy, founded in the Fourteenth Amendment concept of "personal liberty," encompasses the decision to terminate a pregnancy, during the first trimester, without government interference. Nevertheless, the original intent of the framers of the Constitution continues to be debated by legal scholars. Did the framers overlook privacy as an intrinsic right? Or did they intend for the states to make their own determinations?

Where access to information is concerned, says Shaw (2003), "[p]olitical candidates, national and state political parties, the courts, advocacy organizations, pollsters, and the media have dedicated substantial attention to this issue over the past three decades" (407). Even now, when Justice Samuel Alito was first nominated, his stance on *Roe v. Wade* was carefully weighed, as is typically the case with potential and actual Supreme Court nominees. Also, in 2006, the U.S. Food and Drug Administration's (FDA's) controversial decision to make Plan B, the so-called morning-after pill, available only to women over the age of eighteen without a prescription continues to be the subject of substantial debate. According to the Center for Reproductive Rights, 2005 saw twenty-four states enact thirty-nine laws designed to restrict access to abortion.

Despite the level of activity and available information about abortion, public opinion has remained essentially the same for the last thirty years. Two published studies analyzing the results of public opinion polls on abortion from 1977 through 2003 found that "most respondents [in a range of public opinion surveys over the years] say that they have very strong opinions on abortion and that they have not changed their minds in recent years on the issue" (Shaw 2003, 407).

Presumably, it is the complexity, including both its emotional and rational aspects, that allows public opinion to remain murky. As Bowman puts it, "[s]omething really significant has to occur to bring Americans back into the debate" (Benac, 2006). One wonders what that something could possibly be, in light of the fact that information regarding legal and court decisions, murders of abortion providers, and abortion as an issue in political campaigns and the confirmation process does not appear to be significant enough to affect public opinion in a substantial way.

Both abortion and the death penalty share circumstances related to the founding principles of life, liberty, and the pursuit of happiness. The first of these, life, has been used as the basis for the primary argument against abortion—protecting the *life* of the unborn, the *life* of a child—and as the basis for abortion—protecting the *life* of the mother—if only in limited cases. In each case, emphasizing the humanity of the unborn and the mother are substantial components of the rhetoric, as in the phrasing seen in, "It's a child, not a choice." However, a decision that reflects the need to value both the lives of the mother and (potentially) the unborn and liberty, the second principle, is not easily reached. Similarly, a decision that reflects valuing the life of the crime victim and the life of someone who is convicted of the crime and faces the death penalty is also not easy to identify.

The third principle, the pursuit of happiness, resides at the bottom of the hierarchy:

Americans draw sharp distinctions between various motivations and circumstances of pregnant women who seek abortion. Threats to a woman's life and health tend to elicit much stronger support for access, compared with concerns about fetal defects, for instance. Other arguments for abortion, such as financial hardship or simple desire for no more children, find lower levels of support. (Shaw 2003, 413)

While Americans clearly value life, their opinions invariably link it with liberty. This dual focus makes it difficult for Americans to limit the rights of others, whether or not there is agreement regarding the hierarchy and interpretation of those rights.

As indicated, the pro-abortion argument is often framed in the context of choice, particularly a woman's right to choose. However, the Supreme Court decision was not based on the issue of choice but, in fact, that of liberty, specifically, the right to privacy as embodied in the Fourteenth Amendment—the premise being that "personal liberty" includes the right of the individual to end a pregnancy. According to sociologists Strickler and Danigelis,

the ways that views on abortion become aligned with other social attitudes gauges the relative success of these social movements. Pro-choice movement organizations strive to embrace abortion as an element of a broader "rights" framework. . . . On the other hand, the pro-life movement organizations frame abortion as an issue of morality and sanctity of human life, or "family values." (2002, 191)

Where information is concerned, Strickler and Danigelis also note that

[t]o the extent that abortion attitudes have been shaped by social movement organizations, it appears that the pro-life movement has been more successful in framing the abortion issue than has the pro-choice movement. The two social attitude constructs that have become more closely correlated with abortion attitudes are attitudes toward sexuality and belief about the sanctity of life. These are the two central issues that have been emphasized by pro-life media campaigns. The pro-choice movement, on the other hand, has focused on the claims that legal abortion is an entitlement of the right to privacy, that the state should not be coopted by religious views, and that abortion is necessary for gender equality. (2002, 199)

Further,

the mainstream acceptance of feminist principles has not led to increasing approval of abortion, even though the pro-choice movement has attempted to link these two issues. Second, public opinion has moved in the direction of becoming more "progressive" on the two issues that have become aligned with abortion attitudes: belief in the sanctity of human life and sexual liberalism. The net results of these separate trends is that the pro-life movement has had relatively more success in defining the terms of the debate, but that success has not led to broad-based opposition to abortion. (Strickler and Danigelis 2002, 200)

Geoffrey Nunberg, a linguist at the University of California at Berkeley School of Information and author of *Talking Right: How Conservatives Turned Liberalism into a Tax-Raising, Latte-Drinking, Sushi-Eating, Volvo-Driving, New York Times-Reading, Body-Piercing, Hollywood-Loving, Left-Wing Freak Show* (2006), has conducted statistical analyses of political rhetoric in speeches and the media, among others. He found conservatives to be more "linguistically dominant" in framing the nature of the debate, regardless of the issue under discussion, which may explain why abortion is so frequently presented in terms of whether or not one is "pro-life," a traditionally conservative stance. In other words, how the discussion is framed will have an impact on what information is made available, as well as the terminology of the debate.

Time may not define it, but it does inform the law—both legislation and case law. For pro-choice advocates, constitutionally basing *Roe v. Wade* on the Fourteenth Amendment, which provides what many consider to be some of the most open wording in the Constitution or the Amendments, is shaky ground indeed. At that time, the U.S. was coming out of the Vietnam War. And the expansion of presidential powers during times of war, as far back as the Civil War, has always favored security—previously national security, but now also homeland security—over personal privacies and/or civil liberties. But while presidential powers have typically been rolled back as the wars end, the war on terrorism is seemingly open-ended and, as with previous wars, seen as a vehicle for protecting and ensuring our liberty. Thus, whatever reconsiderations are made, at individual and policy levels, they will likely reflect this new context.

While the issues of the death penalty and abortion represent two of the most complex, emotion-laden, and unresolved issues of our time, they are similar in terms of the seriousness and finality of the decisions and the complexity of their underlying complementary and competing principles.

Does access to information enhance decision making or at least make it easier for one (or many) to decide? Human and societal response to important and difficult decisions can be affected by which information is available and also involve strongly held beliefs and societal principles—life and liberty or "mixing moral qualms with support for abortion access," (Shaw 2003, 413) for example. At the same time, the way in which the information is presented—whether in the form of research, news, or popular media—as well as the context in which it is presented, which cultural themes are supported, and who does the presenting do not necessarily impact decision making in different ways.

For example, public opinion regarding abortion, which tends to be stable, can lead to the discussion of other major issues in society, which are not. Members of the general public may decide about their own reproductive choices, participate in service on a jury, or support a political candidate. Yet, for most people, the contexts are quite limited; instead, a number of other issues help to define these phenomena in relation to increased amounts of information, as well as increasing modes and influence of the media.

The impact of the television media in shaping public opinion has been well documented. For example, during the 1960s, the war in Vietnam was the first war for which images were broadcast widely and frequently to homes in the U.S. While photographs, such as those published in *Life*, became an important component of "the war's visual legacy" (Huebner 2005, 151, 157), it was the vivid, moving images of killings, the dead and the injured, and conditions of the troops, supplemented by accounts of reporters or governmental officials of casualties, victories, and campaigns, that had the strongest impact on public opinion and public support for involvement in the war. In fact, this was the period when television networks expanded their evening news broadcasts to a half-hour for the purposes of "allowing more time for coverage of the war in Vietnam" (Huebner 2005, 151).

Similarly, the availability of information via television, in both amount and type shaped public opinion regarding racial discrimination and oppression in the U.S. Prior to the late 1950s and the 1960s, most people outside of the Southern United States were largely unaware of two aspects of the civil rights movement: the extent of the movement against oppression and segregation; and the extent of the resistance to such movements. Here, too, vivid visual images of marches, the use of fire hoses and police dogs, angry taunts during integration attempts, speeches by individuals such as Martin Luther King, Jr., and

Governor George Wallace, and the murders of civil rights workers Michael Schwerner, Andrew Goodman, and James Earl Chaney was the first "ongoing, brought straight to your living room" coverage for many Americans. While the photographs of lynchings, marches, and "Whites Only" signs were vivid, images of blacks and whites together were more powerful.

Today, the Internet has been credited with increasing the amount and types of information which is made available. For example, Trent Lott's comments in support of the then segregationist philosophy of Strom Thurmond went largely unreported by the major broadcast and print media. It was the bloggers (i.e., Weblog writers) who not only reported them but also provided a discussion forum for them. The subsequent coverage by the print and broadcast media, the public response, and the response of other leaders and politicians, including those in Lott's own party, led to his stepping down from his post.

Thus, public opinion has been influenced by the increasing availability of information, in amount and type, though it appears that the more complex and ethically murky the issue, the less there is directness and causality in the relationship between increased information and changing public opinion. Consequently, access to information must be addressed with the understanding that new and additional information may enhance but not change the decisions being made. And, while the nature and the context of the information may be important in framing the discussion, decisions are not always readily changed.

REFERENCES

Baldus, David C., George Woodworth, David Zuckerman, Neil Alan Weiner, and Barbara Broffitt. "Racial Discrimination and the Death Penalty in the Post-Furman Era: An Empirical and Legal Overview, with Recent Findings from Philadelphia." *Cornell Law Review* 83 (1998): 1638–1770.

Benac, Nancy. "Americans 'Contradictory' on Abortion." *The Miami Herald* (March 13, 2006): 7A. Available at http://docs.newsbank.com/openurl?ctx_ver=z39.88-2004&rft_id=info:sid/iw.newsbank.com:NewsBank:MIHB&rft_val_format=info:ofi/fmt:kev:mtx:ctx&rft_dat=

1105F98969381020&svc_dat=InfoWeb:aggregated5&req_dat=
0FF0DDC272369ADF (accessed January 31, 2008).

Bohm, Robert M. "American Death Penalty Opinion: Past, Present, and Future." In *America's Experiment with Capital Punishment*. Edited by James R. Acker, Robert M. Bohm, and Charles S. Lanier. Durham, NC: Carolina Academic Press, 1998.

————. "American Death Penalty Opinion: Past, Present, and Future." In *America's Experiment with Capital Punishment*. Second edition. Edited by James R. Acker, Robert M. Bohm, and Charles S. Lanier. Durham, NC: Carolina Academic Press, 2003.

Cochran, John K., and Mitchell B. Chamlin. "Can Information Change Public Opinion? Another Test of the Marshall Hypotheses." *Journal of Criminal Justice* 33 (2005): 573–584.

Godfried, Nathan. "Identity, Power, and Local Television: African Americans, Organized Labor and UHF-TV in Chicago, 1962–1968." *Historical Journal of Film, Radio and Television* 22 (June 2002): 117–134.

Huebner, Andrew J. "Rethinking American Press Coverage of the Vietnam War, 1965–68." *Journalism History* 31 (Fall 2005): 150–161.

Nunberg, Geoffrey. *Talking Right: How Conservatives Turned Liberalism into a Tax-Raising, Latte-Drinking, Sushi-Eating, Volvo-Driving, New York Times-Reading, Body-Piercing, Hollywood-Loving, Left-Wing Freak Show*. Cambridge, MA: Perseus Books Group, 2006.

Sabet, Kevin A. "Making it Happen: The Case for Compromise in the Federal Cocaine Law Debate." *Social Policy & Administration* 39 (April 2005): 181–191.

Shaw, Greg M. "The Polls—Trends: Abortion." *Public Opinion Quarterly* 67 (Fall 2003): 407–429.

Strickler, Jennifer, and Nicholas L. Danigelis. "Changing Frameworks in Attitudes toward Abortion." *Sociological Forum* 17 (June 2002): 187–201.

Tyler, Tom R. "Viewing *CSI* and the Threshold of Guilt: Managing Truth and Justice in Reality and Fiction." *Yale Law Journal* 115(5) (March 2006). Available at http://www.yalelawjournal.org/pdf/115-5/Tyler.pdf (accessed August 26, 2006).

CHAPTER 4
An Ethics Crisis

The state of ethical decision making might be termed a crisis, with troubling examples in the corporate, educational, and academic communities. From the individual to the organizational levels and even internationally, both actual and potential ethical lapses loom large. Private sector corporate cases have received significant attention and have been the focus of attempts at legislative and regulatory reform, as well as self-regulation. While cases involving political leaders have also received attention, they have engendered less regulation and legislative reform. No profession or sector is immune, not even young people in K-12 and university settings.

Generally speaking, an explanation for the current ethics crisis is our increasingly competitive environment, where prominent figures justify their behavior at any cost. In addition, the determination of what is legal (or not legal) may be narrower or more limited than what is ethical. Nor does it help that making ethical decisions is often less intuitive than we would like to believe.

For the most part, corporate cases are related in particular to inaccurate reporting of financial performance; overstated stock performance and anticipated return on investment, in attempts to influence stock prices and stockholder confidence; inflated executive compensation, particularly in instances of poor organizational performance overall; and, defrauding and/or overcharging institutional and individual customers. While the focus of highly publicized cases, such as Enron, Tyco, Worldcom, Arthur Anderson, and Hollinger, is often senior management, the problem extends to all levels in organizations. According to *The Cheating Culture*, published in 2004, managers and other employees "steal $600 billion from their companies each year" (Winik 2004, 20).

Instances of ethics cases and investigations involving politicians at the national level are legion. Former House Majority Leader Tom Delay was admonished by the House Ethics Committee and indicted by a grand jury in Texas for activities related to fundraising irregularities. Other high-profile cases have included those of Senate Majority Leader Bill Frist and U.S. Representatives Duke Cunningham of California, Bob Ney of Ohio, and William Jefferson of Louisiana. In the case of Frist, he "sold stock in his family's hospital company one month before its price fell sharply" (Birnbaum and Smith 2005, A01), thus raising questions about whether he engaged in insider trading. There was no real legal conclusion, as the situation appeared to end with the allegation. In 2005, Randy "Duke" Cunningham resigned from Congress "after pleading guilty to taking more than $2 million in bribes in a criminal conspiracy involving at least three defense contractors" (CNN.com 2005). As part of "the influence-peddling investigation of lobbyist Jack Abramoff," Representative Bob Ney "admitted performing official acts for lobbyists in exchange for campaign contributions, expensive meals, luxury travel and skybox sports tickets. Ney also admitted taking thousands of dollars in gambling chips from an international businessman who sought his help with the State Department" (Schmidt and Grimaldi 2006). William Jefferson, who was reelected to Congress in 2006, was investigated for taking bribes. His Capitol Hill office was searched, and FBI agents found $90,000 in cash in the freezer in his home. In 2007, he was served with a "16-count indictment, including allegations of money laundering, bribery and racketeering, [representing] . . . the first charges ever brought against a U.S. official for violating the Foreign Corrupt Practices Act, enacted 30 years ago to combat bribery of foreign officials by U.S. corporations" (Schmitt and Simmons 2007, A1).

The criminal cases against public figures other than politicians tend to proceed quickly. For example, Lobbyist Jack Abramoff immediately pleaded guilty to charges of attempted bribery, as did the defense contractor who bribed Cunningham. Perhaps out of self-interest, politicians exhibit serious difficulty in passing ethics reform legislation at either the state or national levels and are clearly ill at ease when responding to ethical investigations of their own colleagues. Most notably, in the case of the ethics investigation involving William Jefferson, the FBI search of "Jefferson's quarters in the Rayburn House Office Building posed a new political dilemma for the leaders of both parties, who felt compelled to protest his treatment while condemning any wrongdoing by the lawmaker" (Eggen and Murray 2006, A01).

In addition to the instances involving lobbyists and politicians, other such cases of ethical abuses occur at the intersection between the private and the public sectors. In what has become known as war profiteering, contractors have been accused of taking advantage of relationships with elected officials and officials in government agencies in securing contracts, as well as taking advantage of the availability of resources associated with military and rebuilding efforts. In this regard, "[t]he first civil fraud case against a U.S. contractor accused of war profiteering in Iraq" (Babcock 2006, D01) was reported in 2006. In the case, involving the company Custer Battles, LLC, accusations involved "overcharging the government millions of dollars by running inflated expense billings through a series of shell companies they created" (Ibid.). Court documents have been particularly revealing in the case, with a "spreadsheet showing the company's actual expenses and much higher figures for what it was charging the government" (Ibid.). In addition, the case was of interest because the Coalition Provisional Authority in Iraq (CPA) "has been criticized for failing to properly oversee the spending of more than $20 billion in U.S. reconstruction funds. . . . [Documentation has indicated that] financial systems were so shoddy that billions of dollars couldn't be accounted for" (Ibid.). Further highlighting fault in the public sector, "[c]ourt filings in the Custer Battles case detail how CPA officials in Baghdad were ill-equipped to write, much less oversee, the processing of millions of dollars in contracts. For example, the agency couldn't wire money to Custer Battles and its contractors, so it sometimes advanced them millions of dollars in cash, according to the records" (Ibid.).

While the Custer Battles case is noteworthy, it is by no means the only one. There have been highly publicized cases of companies taking advantage of contract and resource availability, including the infamous cases of amounts spent by agencies on screwdrivers and toilet seats and cases involving contracts associated with the rebuilding efforts after Hurricane Katrina. It would seem that ethical leadership requires decision making that reflects the efficient and appropriate use of resources; conversely, waste, excess, and ineffectiveness represent unethical behavior, as does outright fraud and misrepresentation.

Although the focus of the research and discussion of ethical decision making is primarily the private sector and public officials, challenges are not limited to those arenas alone. For example, nonprofit organizations, including the United Way and the American Red Cross, have been the subject of ethics investigations, as well. In college sports, for example, investigations of high-profile recruitment scandals have been reported in a number of institutions (Jacobson 2004, 1–3), in many instances, linking the scandals to poor management, including vague and incomplete policy statements, and lack of oversight by those in authority.

Nor do young people themselves make individual decisions in a vacuum but are influenced by a number of forces, including their sense of what others are doing, what is necessary in order to be competitive, and what their role models do and say. Not surprisingly, the results of self-report research indicate that three-quarters of high school students admit to having cheated (Winik 2004, 20). Such a statistic is troubling yet almost understandable: "While this surge has been blamed on many factors, including a declining emphasis on moral values in the home and school, without question it's never been easier to cheat" (Barr 2000). Thus, the sheer availability of information, seemingly open to all, results in "a treasure-trove of information they can pinch without proper attribution" (Ibid.). Similarly, technological advances, particularly the Internet and portable electronic devices, aid and abet such activities.

However, another aspect of the societal context appears to be of importance, as well. According to Gay Jervey, author of "Cheating: But Everybody's Doing It" (2000), "[a] bigger factor, though, is the way bad behavior across society—ballplayers popping steroids, business executives cooking corporate books, journalists fabricating quotes, even teachers faking test scores to make schools look good—signals that nothing is out of bounds when success is at stake." Similarly, there is a lack of contrition or a sense that ethical behavior is important or necessary.

Lastly, the issue of cheating appears to be complicated by cultural factors. In a highly publicized 2007 case, thirty-four MBA students at Duke University were found guilty of "cheat[ing] on a take-home final exam, a judicial board has found, in what officials called the most widespread cheating episode in the business school's history" (Finder 2007, 15). The specifics of the case involved "an open-book test in a required course in March, with students told to take the exam on their own. But many students collaborated, in violation of the school's honor code" (Ibid.). While the penalties for those found guilty by the school's judicial board ranged from expulsions and suspensions to failing grades in the class and on the exam, an attorney for sixteen of the students noted that the majority of the students found guilty were Asian. In this regard, concerns related to an understanding of the nature of collaboration and attribution in academic work in the U.S., as well as understanding of the review process associated with violations, were raised. Attorney Robert Ekstrand has suggested that the cheating

primarily involved students in the United States less than a year and who did not understand the honor code or judicial proceedings well. . . . Violations were minor, Ekstrand said. But when a faculty investigator pressured them to admit wrongdoing, they quickly wrote contrite letters of confession, some- times without knowing the specifics of the accusation, he said. Swift hearings and convictions followed. (Stancill 2007, 5)

And, the nature of the judicial process and the confessions disadvan- taged the students, according to the attorney, suggesting that "[b]ecause the students pleaded guilty, their hearings were brief and they were not able to explain to the judicial board the particulars of what they did and didn't do (Ibid.). In this regard, "[c]ultural norms led the students, who come from Asian countries including China, Korea and Taiwan, to express shame and remorse instead of fighting the charges, the lawyer said. 'Culturally, a confession or an admission of guilt can be a way to apologize,' he said" (Ibid).

The ethical abuses of senior managers and other high-level decision makers in the public and the private sectors and other arenas have re- ceived press coverage and are the topic of public scrutiny. However, the preceding list of examples, while not nearly exhaustive, is illustrative of the fact that the problem is far more widespread and pervasive.

The nature of the research presented in *The Cheating Culture* is reflected in an astonishing number of competitive arenas. Professional and amateur sports are no exception. In the case of athletes who have been accused of and/or admitted to the use of performance-enhancing drugs, there is the supposition that such tactics are necessary in order to compete and certainly to be exceptional. The effects of more widespread use (alleged or otherwise) of performance-enhancing drugs have been multifaceted. For example, the situation has led to questioning the credibility and performance of many of sports' highest-achieving athletes, including baseball player Barry Bonds, Olympic runner Justin Gatlin, and cyclist and 2006 Tour de France winner, Floyd Landis. At the same time, the number of athletes who have tested positive for performance-enhancing drugs has been so substantial that such frequently mentioned examples are vivid but not unique, and the integrity of entire sports, as diverse as cycling, track and field, and baseball have been questioned (Quinn 2004). In track and field, Olympic champion Marion Jones was convicted of making false statements "to federal investigators in November 2003, acknowledging she took the designer steroid 'the clear' from September 2000 to July 2001. 'The clear' has been linked to BALCO, the lab at the center of the steroids scandal in professional sports" (Fitzgerald 2008). In addition, "Jones returned her [five] Olympic medals . . . even before the International Olympic Committee ordered her to do so and wiped her results from the books" (Ibid.). In the case of cycling, the World Anti-Doping Agency was formed in 1999 in response to the International Olympic Committee's concern over cycling competition in 1998 and in preparation for the Sydney Olympics in 2000. While Landis is a recent and high-profile example, a number of top cyclists were withdrawn before the 2006 race for having tested positive in the past. According to an article entitled "Vast Doping Scandal Puts Cycling at a Fork in Road," "[t]he unprecedented scope (implicating 58 cyclists) and dramatic timing of this crackdown may also set a new standard for other sports dogged by allegations of illegal drug use" (Case and Sachs 2006). The president of the World Anti-Doping Agency was quoted as saying, "Either this is the worst day in the history of cycling or it's the day when they finally start getting a handle on the problems" (Ibid.). In auto racing, 2007 may "be known as the year of the cheat." With five instances of cheating identified in vehicle inspections in relation to the first race of the season, the Daytona 500, NASCAR (National Association for Stock Car Auto Racing) handed down "some of the harshest penalties in series history." Alleged offenses included the use of "an illegal additive . . . [I]ts intent was to aid performance illegally." Similar offenses, designed to enhance aerodynamics, included questionable modifications to vehicles, such as "holes in the wheel wells . . . [that] were not sealed as required" (Bernstein 2007a). In all of the instances, the tactics appear to violate the association's rules, in attempts to enhance performance.

Given the prevalence of such proven cases, allegations, and suspicion, exceptional performances that surpass what has been achieved in the past have both raised the bar in terms of present and future performance and made older records that are broken or likely to be broken all the more sacred (and, according to Wilbon, have led to the question of adding an "asterisk" to records achieved in an era of steroids) (2004). As well, the prevailing belief that cheating is the norm is likely to encourage further cheating. In the win-at-all-costs model, character is less the basis for measuring success than is achievement.

Even society's views of success and top performers—including record breakers—are a representation of a societal change; so are the examples of attempts to regulate and provide punishment for such offenses. As a clear indication of the increased evidence of use of performance-enhancing drugs and the efforts to crack down on such use, a first occurred during the 2006 Winter Olympics. "Police never before had raided Olympians in a doping investigation. The IOC [International Olympic Committee] triggered the operation by relaying to Italian authorities a tip from the World Anti-Doping Agency on Mayer's [a ski coach from Austria who has been linked to doping queries] activities" (Hohler 2006, D2). In fact, "police investigations—rather than testing by sports authorities—have so far proved the most effective way to catch cheaters" (Case and Sachs 2006).

The perceived lack of individual and corporate responsibility has led to federal-level and statewide attempts to provide regulation and criminal penalties for unethical behavior across the private, nonprofit, and public sectors. Activities of some key players in the Enron case, in particular, which have been described as "not illegal," are more revealing of limitations in the law, at least prior to 2002, than of broadly defined ethical standards. Regulation has come in the form of enhanced oversight and reporting requirements by the Securities and Exchange Commission and federal legislation, such as the Sarbanes-Oxley Act of 2002. Its purpose is to provide more specific requirements for senior managers to take responsibility for the financial reporting, as an accurate representation of company performance and financial strength, and avoid the deleterious effects of "overly powerful CEOs, weak boards and audit committees, ineffective or compliant auditors, weak internal controls and weak management of risks, and soft penalties for accounting fraud perpetrators" (Beasley 2004, 11).

A key premise of Sarbanes-Oxley is the fact that preventing fraud is, in and of itself, a good thing, and that shareholders (and employees), particularly in publicly traded companies, require access to accurate and certified information regarding the purchase and sale of stock. "Under the requirements of the Sarbanes-Oxley Act, executives must personally certify a public company's financial results (section 302) and . . . issue a report on the effectiveness of the company's internal controls over financial reporting (section 404)" (Ibid.). "In addition, it addresses the issue of separation of powers between CEOs and their boards and attempts to ensure auditor accountability, specifically with auditor independence (section 201), audit committee composition (section 301), and criminal penalties for accounting fraud and related offenses (Title VIII and Title IX)" (Ibid.).

The issue of increased regulation in the for-profit sector is evidenced in not only the passing of Sarbanes-Oxley but also in the criminal phase of the Enron case, which has become symbolic of corporate corruption. The jurors' verdict and explanation regarding the verdict reflect the fact that their intent was not only to decide the case but also to send a message regarding the corruption and the lack of contrition in causing harm to hardworking, trusting employees. As a juror put it after the trial, "I performed my duty as an American citizen. I've never fought on a foreign battleground (but) I fought on this battleground for American justice" (Pasha and Said 2006). Similarly, after the verdict was announced, the Deputy U.S. Attorney General Paul McNulty indicated that other corporate executives should take the verdict as a warning and an indication of the Department of Justice's intent to pursue subsequent cases vigorously. Lead government prosecutor Sean Berkowitz added, "The eyes of the world have been on this courthouse and they have seen the justice system at work. . . . No matter how rich you are, you have to play by the rules" (Ibid.).

Both Sarbanes-Oxley and enhanced enforcement by the SEC have focused on the threat of financial penalties; in a climate consisting of a range of activities, some of which were not illegal before the passage of Sarbanes-Oxley, there appears to be a presumption or conclusion that doing the right thing requires motivation and often the threat of repercussions for failing to do so.

While there have been attempts at self-regulation in the private sector, movement towards the separation of powers of the CEO and chair of corporate board positions has been slow (Iwata 2004, 4B). However, increased emphasis on organizational and professional codes of ethics has provided a basis for individual and organizational decision making (Hatcher 2003, 42–45).

Beyond the private sector, the nonprofit sector has attempted to preempt or forestall legislation and greater oversight by increasing the level of self-regulation, for example through certification. At the government level, the Senate Finance Committee has considered "legislation to tighten nonprofit oversight and require charities to re-apply for nonprofit status every five years" (Salmon 2004, C1).

While attempts at regulation and punishment are necessary for responding to and deterring unethical behavior, it is important to understand the basis for such behavior. As a society, we acknowledge the presence and prevalence of unethical behavior, even as we value ethical practice and want to see justice. This attitude drives much of the immigration debate, where the "path to citizenship" is strewn with concerns over rewarding (or not punishing) those who are guilty of illegal behavior. In the case of NASCAR, for example, Brian France, NASCAR's chairman and chief executive, has indicated the need to foster integrity in the sport by punishing those who break the rules and to "step up the penalties to a level that makes it a true deterrent" (Bernstein 2007b).

In a world of Enron and Olympic doping, how do we encourage ethical decision making and ethical leadership? If the goal is for the individual's ability to make ethical decisions to be on par with his or her desire to do so, preparation is clearly needed; exhibiting integrity is a competency that can be developed but which is not necessarily an innate behavior. In fact, quite a number of factors are working against ethical decision making. While organizations, lawmakers, and policy-makers have offered responses and potential deterrents for unethical behavior, the research related to ethical decision making indicates that there are a number of factors that serve as motivators for unethical behavior and complicate the process of making ethical decisions: the nature of competition in the current climate, the ways in which success and performance are viewed, and the lack of educational preparation for ethical decision making.

In an increasingly competitive environment, for both organizations and individuals, there are conflicting priorities associated with being successful in relation to competitors and the market overall, with the potential financial rewards, which may be substantial. Thus, it may be difficult to make ethical choices if success is less immediate in relation to competitors. In this regard, Callahan makes a compelling argument as to the existence of a phenomenon known as the "cheating effect," i.e., the supposition that others are cheating causes one to engage in unethical behavior, as well, in order to be competitive (2004).

In addition to powerful motivators associated with competition and successful performance, the research also indicates that making ethical decisions is not only a matter of the will to do so. The desire and the will may be overshadowed by the lack of preparation, ability, and awareness of the impact of unconscious bias and influence of the external environment on ethical decision making. In fact, research related to ethical decision making indicates that many people—managers in organizations, in particular—overestimate their ability to make ethical decisions. "More than two decades of research confirms that, in reality, most of us fall woefully short of our inflated self-perception" (Banaji, Bazerman, and Chugh 2003, 56). Thus, the individual must acknowledge the potential lack of awareness regarding his or her own biases and the impact of those biases in decision making.

Ultimately, ethics education should provide a basis for preparing graduates to be successful performers and ethical decision makers and leaders. The importance of ethics education has been identified by those in K-12, university, and graduate and professional education. As might be expected, business schools have been at the forefront of the attempt to incorporate ethics education into their curricula. However, as business school faculty have expressed concerns about how best to make ethics a part of their degree programs, in the development and delivery of curricula, other disciplines have and will continue to face similar questions. In providing a sound basis in preparation for the range of decisions that graduates, employees, and members of society face, ethics education provides the opportunity for the exposure to content and decision making techniques and also to help individuals to be more conscious of the need to make ethical decisions.

REFERENCES

"Affidavit: $90,000 Found in Congressman's Freezer." CNN.com (May 22, 2006). Available at http://www.cnn.com/2006/POLITICS/05/21/jefferson.search/index.html (accessed April 18, 2007).

Ariel, David "Austrian Ski Coach Acknowledges Suicide Attempt." *The Providence Journal* (February 22, 2006). Available at http://www.projo.com/sharedcontent/sports/olympics/LatestNews/news-cw/022206ccwcSportsOLYaustriaskicoach.5103921a.html (accessed February 2, 2008).

Babcock, Charles R. "Contractor Fraud Trial to Begin Tomorrow." *The Washington Post* (February 13, 2006): D01.

Banaji, Mahzarin R., Max H. Bazerman, and Dolly Chugh. "How (Un)Ethical Are You?" *Harvard Business Review* 81(12) (December 2003): 56–64.

Barr, Stephen. "Let's Put the Heat on Campus Cheats: The Scandal of College Cheating." *Reader's Digest* (May 2000). Available at http://www.rd.com/content/openContent.do?contentId=17939&trkid=rdcom_ntscp (accessed April 10, 2006).

Barrett, Ted. "House Ethics Committee Admonishes DeLay Again." CNN.com (October 7, 2004). Available at http://www.cnn.com/2004/ALLPOLITICS/10/07/delay.ethics/ (accessed April 14, 2006).

Beasley, Mark S. "Going Beyond Sarbanes-Oxley Compliance: Five Keys to Creating Value." *The CPA Journal* 74 (6) (June 2004): 11–13.

Bernstein, Viv (a). "Nascar Ejects Waltrip's Crew Chief." *The New York Times* (February 15, 2007). Available at http://www.nytimes.com/2007/02/15/sports/othersports/15nascar.html?ex=1329282000&en=1e722cae76e654d8&ei=5124&partner=permalink&exprod=permalink (accessed January 31, 2008).

Bernstein, Viv (b). "Nascar Makes Aggressive Move against Cheating." *The New York Times* (February 14, 2007). Available at http://www.nytimes.com/2007/02/14/sports/othersports/14nascar.html?ex=1329195600&en=24d9462eaa33f89a&ei=5124&partner=permalink&exprod=permalink (accessed January 31, 2008).

Birnbaum, Jeffrey, and R. Jeffrey Smith. "SEC, Justice Investigate Frist's Sale of Stock." *The Washington Post* (September 24, 2005): A01. Available at http://www.washingtonpost.com/wp-dyn/content/article/2005/09/23/AR2005092301811.html (accessed April 14, 2006).

Callahan, David. *The Cheating Culture: Why More Americans Are Doing Wrong to Get Ahead.* Orlando, FL: Harcourt, Inc., 2004.

Case, Christa, and Susan Sachs. "Vast Doping Scandal Puts Cycling at a Fork in Road." *The Christian Science Monitor* (July 3, 2006). Available at http://www.csmonitor.com/2006/0703/p01s02-woeu.html?s=widep (accessed September 2, 2006).

"Congressman Resigns after Bribery Plea." CNN.com (November 28, 2005). Available at http://www.cnn.com/2005/POLITICS/11/28/cunningham/ (accessed April 18, 2007).

Curtius, Mary. "Senators Set to Begin Push for Ethics Office." *Los Angeles Times* (March 2, 2006): A15.

"DeLay Conspiracy Charges Tossed, Money Laundering Case Remains." FOXNews.com (December 6, 2005). Available at http://www.foxnews.com/story/0,2933,177753,00.html (accessed April 14, 2006).

Eggen, Dan, and Shailagh Murray. "FBI Raid on Lawmaker's Office Is Questioned: Democrat Jefferson Denies Wrongdoing." *The Washington Post* (May 28, 2006): A01. Available at http://www.washingtonpost.com/wp-dyn/content/article/2006/05/22/AR2006052201080.html (accessed August 27, 2006).

Finder, Allan. "34 Duke Business Students Face Discipline for Cheating." *The New York Times* (May 1, 2007): A15.

Fisher, Ian. "2 Athletes Worried They Broke Law." *The New York Times* (February 22, 2006) Available at http://www.nytimes.com/2006/02/22/sports/olympics/22drugs.html (accessed January 31, 2008).

Fitzgerald, Jim. "Marion Jones, Olympic Champ, Sentenced to 6 Months for Lying." *The Seattle Times* (January 12, 2008) Available at http://seattletimes.nwsource.com/html/sports/2004119963_webjones11.html (accessed February 6, 2008).

Hatcher, Tim. "New World Ethics." *Training & Development* 57(8) (August 2003): 42–45.

Hohler, Bob. "Austrian Officials Decry Mayer; Actions by Central Figure of Raid Are 'Inexcusable.'" *The Boston Globe* (February 21, 2006): D2.

Iwata, Edward. "To Split, or Not to Split? That Is The Question Shareholders Are Raising." *USA Today* (March 17, 2004): 4B.

Jacobson, Jennifer. "Panel Blasts U. of Colorado for Handling of Scandal." *The Chronicle of Higher Education*, 50(38) (May 28, 2004): 1–3.

Jervey, Gay. "Cheating: 'But Everybody's Doing It.'" *Reader's Digest* (March 2006). Available at http://www.rd.com/content/openContent.do?contentId=25419 (accessed April 10, 2006).

Pasha, Shaheen, and Jessica Said. "Lay and Skilling's Day of Reckoning: Enron Ex-CEO and Founder Convicted on Fraud and Conspiracy Charges; Sentencing Slated for September." CNNMoney.com (May

25, 2006). Available at http://money.cnn.com/2006/05/25/news/newsmakers/enron_verdict/ (accessed June 5, 2006).

Quinn, T. J. "Tainted Legacy: Steroid Cloud Hangs over Flo-Jo, Golden Age of Women's Track and Field." *Daily News* (July 3, 2004). Available at http://www.nydailynews.com/archives/sports/2004/07/04/2004-07-04_tainted_legacy_steroid_cloud.html (accessed January 31, 2008).

Rojstaczer, Stuart. "Where All Grades Are Above Average." *The Washington Post* (January 28, 2003): A21. Available at http://www.washingtonpost.com/ac2/wp-dyn?pagename=article&node=&contentId=A52648-2003Jan27&notFound=true (accessed August 28, 2006).

Salmon, Jacqueline L. "Nonprofit Endorsements Will Expand." *The Washington Post* (June 27, 2004): C1.

Schmidt, Susan, and James V. Grimaldi. "Ney Pleads Guilty to Corruption Charges." *The Washington Post* (October 14, 2006). Available at http://www.washingtonpost.com/wp-dyn/content/article/2006/10/13/AR2006101300169.html (accessed April 18, 2007).

Schmitt, Richard B., and Ann Simmons. "Jefferson Indicted on Graft Charges; The Democrat from Louisiana Allegedly Solicited Millions for Himself and His Family." *Los Angeles Times* (June 5, 2007): A1.

Smith, R. Jeffrey. "DeLay Indicted in Texas Finance Probe." *The Washington Post* (September 29, 2005): A01. Available at http://www.washingtonpost.com/wp-dyn/content/article/2005/09/28/AR2005092800270.html (accessed April 14, 2006).

Smith, R. Jeffrey, and Jonathan Weisman. "DeLay's Felony Charge Is Upheld: But Texas Judge Dismissed Some Conspiracy Counts." *The Washington Post* (December 6, 2005): A01. Available at http://www.washingtonpost.com/wp-dyn/content/article/2005/12/05/AR2005120500426.html (accessed April 14, 2006).

Stancill, Jane. "Most of Punished Students Are Asian; Lawyer for Accused at Duke Points to Cultural Differences." *The News & Observer* (May 22, 2007): 5.

Thomma, Steven. "One Nation, Divided By Clash of Values: Morality Disputes That Marked Race for President Continue Unabated." *The Sunday Star-Ledger* (December 19, 2004): 37.

"Tom DeLay's Transgressions: A Pattern of Misbehavior." Common Cause. Available at http://www.commoncause.org/site/pp.asp?c=dkLNK1MQIwG&b=476747 (accessed April 14, 2006).

"Travel Agency Subpoenaed for DeLay Records." *The Washington Post* (March 2, 2006): A04. Available at http://www.washingtonpost.com/wp-dyn/content/article/2006/03/01/AR2006030102749.html (accessed April 14, 2006).

Wilbon, Michael. "Tarnished Records Deserve an Asterisk." *The Washington Post* (December 4, 2004): D10. Available at http://docs.newsbank.com/openurl?ctx_ver=z39.88-2004&rft_id=info:sid/iw.newsbank.com:NewsBank:WPIW&rft_val_format=info:ofi/fmt:kev:mtx:ctx&rft_dat=106C6893357D209E&svc_dat=InfoWeb:aggregated5&req_dat=0FF0DDC272369ADF (accessed February 4, 2008).

Winik, Lyric Wallwork. "Are We a Nation of Cheaters?" *PARADE* (March 28, 2004): 20.

CHAPTER 5
Decision Making

The ability to make informed and ethical decisions is dependent on the information to which one has access, the level and extent to which one has been prepared, and the context in which both the information and the decision will be applied. However, as discussed in Chapters 2 and 3, the amount of information that is made easily available by others is not the only basis for more refined decision making. There is also the need to be proactive in seeking access to useful information of quality and in increasing awareness and acknowledgement of variations in quality and reflections of bias in the sources of information and in oneself as a decision maker. Young people, in particular, are often considered to be poor or ill-prepared and easily influenced in making decisions, often by negative forces, and likely to be impulsive and emotional and unwilling to seek advice or information from reputable sources.

Accordingly, the decision making process involves more than simply identifying an issue or problem and selecting what appears to be an appropriate solution. It must also take into consideration: the context in which the decision is being made; an analysis of the issue or problem, beyond its symptoms; identification of alternative courses of action, along with the potential implications of each alternative; and a rationale for defining success.

Research into leadership competencies has revealed common qualities, areas of knowledge, and abilities possessed by successful leaders, such as "adaptability, effective interpersonal communication, and good decision making" (Barner 2000, 51; Intagliata, Ulrich, and Smallwood 2000), including the importance of integrity, specifically when dealing with difficult ethical questions. Together, they indicate the types of educational preparation and subsequent professional development needed by leaders.

Young people, in particular, are likely to be influenced by those for whom they have respect and admiration, role models who reflect what is necessary to succeed and, secondarily, what is appropriate, acceptable, or possible. Corporate executives, for example, who have been successful, through making ethically questionable choices, give the impression that cheating in one form or another is the norm. The research which supports these contentions is troubling, as well as compelling, indicating that role models are not necessarily those who have made ethical choices but potentially those who win at any cost.

While many young people look to athletes for examples of successful performance, it is compounded by high-profile examples, in professional, college, and amateur contexts, of those who have been involved in cases ranging from domestic abuse and sexual assault to illegal gambling and the use of performance-enhancing drugs. The issue is further complicated by what appears to be support for this questionable behavior by those with the responsibility for setting and maintaining organizational and professional standards, including coaches, university administrators, and Olympic officials. The apparent support for athletes by these responsible parties suggests a level of validation for their (documented or alleged) unethical behavior and, possibly, a double standard for those who are successful or who have the potential for success. Lastly, successful athletes do not benefit only themselves, such that those who make the most money for the team are more valued and consequently worthy of being judged by a different standard.

The impact of athletes as role models is also a function of media proliferation. According to researchers Brown, Basil, and Bocarnea, "[t]he international proliferation of entertainment media during the past two decades has provided unprecedented public access to knowledge about the lives of celebrities" (2003, 42). However, in addition to providing greater scrutiny of the lives, behavior, and decision making of the famous, this increase in media coverage has affected perceptions of them, to the extent that "celebrities have replaced the traditional heroes of the past" (Ibid., 43).

Concurrent with the societal shift in how we identify our heroes is a corresponding shift in the criteria by which we identify and evaluate them. In the past, role models were by and large parents, relatives, and neighbors—those who were personally known in their communities and who epitomized courage and moral character. The research indicates that "[p]arents are arguably the most important adults in the lives of most children. Parents have significant effects on their children's development of beliefs, goals, attitudes, and behaviors, as well as on other aspects of the individual" (Beam, Chen, and Greenberger 2002, 305–306). As children get older and "make the transition into adolescence, however, they come into contact with a broader array of adults" (Ibid., 306). While the impact of parental influence is not eliminated but diminished somewhat, "[s]tudies of young people's ties to non-parental adults—sometimes kin, sometimes others—have shown . . . that nonparental adults may exert a strong influence on psychosocial adjustment" (Ibid.). Thus, young people note that parents and other family members and adults, including teachers, with whom they have personal relationships are the most influential role models in their lives.

However, while the research continues to reflect the importance of these traditional adults as role models, their level of influence is changing, as they compete with more remote and potentially more successful, larger-than-life role models, who, because they "are seldom known personally . . . are not required by the public to possess any virtue other than being well-known and having outstanding talent" (Brown, Basil, and Bocarnea 2003, 43).

Thus, it appears that in identifying and evaluating heroes, the bar is higher in terms of extraordinary performance, skill, and celebrity and not as high in terms of character. As a result, "[i]t is much easier today to disregard or overlook moral failures in leaders who accomplish good works in a society that worships fame than in a society that honors heroes for both achievement and moral character" (Ibid.). In addition, while most young people will not achieve fame or success as athletes, the idea of "overlooking moral failures in leaders who accomplish good works in a society that worships fame" could certainly be interpreted broadly in the corporate or other professional contexts in which "good works" are equated to successful, if not ethical, performance.

It is important to note that the research shows that as role models, athletes do have influence. According to Brown, Basil, and Bocarnea, "[a]lthough the influence of sports celebrities on behavior needs much more scholarly examination, there are a number of studies that indicate that famous people can effectively persuade others to purchase products and adopt certain health-related beliefs and practices" (2003, 44). In this regard, the media serves to create a perceived relationship between the viewer and the celebrity, such that "parasocial interaction" results. "Audience members commonly look to media personalities as 'friends' and those with whom they feel 'comfortable'" (Ibid., 46). This happens via "a process of cognitive, affective, and behavioral participation that occurs while actively responding to media presentations" (Ibid.). With athletes, in particular, the level of exposure is substantial, with both live and televised sporting events, movies, and commercials. As early as the 1960s, researchers such as Kelman addressed the concept of "identification." "In this identification process, a person adopts attitudes, values and behaviors of another because he or she actually believes in them, and it is not necessary that the person 'role modeling' the behavior of another actually interacts with the 'role model'" (Ibid., 47).

To what extent are young people more or differently susceptible to the influence of others than are adults? Clearly, there is complexity associated with the decision making of young people. The question of the influence of role models appears to be addressed if not answered fully in the research related to the complexity of romantic relationships between young people and teachers. Such relationships are not new. However, most research has focused mainly on university settings, raising questions related to the maturation process, the differences in cognitive and emotional development among individual young people, and the potential impact of authority figures in influencing the decision making process. Despite the growing number of high-profile cases of such relationships between teachers and K-12 students, there is very little scholarly research related to adolescent-teacher romantic relationships. Many of the teachers involved in such relationships have suggested that the relationships are not only consensual, suggesting informed decision making by themselves and the students, but also that the involvement represents a relationship of equals or peers. According to experts, the teachers hold the balance of power, making such relationships inherently unequal.

The fact that there is such limited research associated with sexual and/or romantic relationships between teachers and middle or high school students is likely based on a number of factors, including the relatively recent press coverage of such cases in the United States, societal taboos, and the related challenges of receiving approval from university boards that oversee research on human subjects in the case of such delicate topics that would likely involve interviews with young people.

The research related to similar relationships among faculty and college students does address the nature of influence, noting that students who are older are presumably better able to make informed decisions than is the case with middle or high school students. However, researchers disagree when the varying circumstances come into play.

For example, Ann Pellegrini has addressed the importance of acknowledging the potential for relationship building between adults, with the consent of the student. She has noted that, in the current context of sexual harassment guidelines in higher education, "[i]ncreasingly, universities have come to amend their sexual harassment policies to include so-called third party allegations of sexual harassment" (1999, 617). In this regard, "the most frequent focus of this intensified regulatory attention is consensual sexual relationships between faculty and students" (Ibid.). Pellegrini contends that terminology such as "alleged consensual relationships" goes beyond acknowledging the potential power dynamics in such relationships, to negate the possibility of voluntary consent on the part of the student. As Jane Gollop has noted, it "does not merely qualify what counts as consent; it disqualifies the possibility of consent altogether" (1997, 35). Both Pellegrini and Gollop are concerned with the gendered aspect of the interpretation of sexual harassment in this context, whereby the woman, as student and victim, is portrayed without the ability to consent.

However, Virginia Lee Stamler and Gerald L. Stone's 1998 book *Faculty-Student Sexual Involvement* takes the stance that

[t]he student and faculty member both may view the relationship as one between two consenting adults, but relationships between professionals and those whom they serve contain an inherent power imbalance. A student cannot enter into a sexual relationship with a faculty member as an equal. Can a

student ignore the status of the professor or the admiration she or he may have for her or his position? Is it possible to ignore the power the professor may have over her or his current education or future career? (11–12)

In citing the work of Marilyn Peterson on professional-client relationships (1992), Stamler and Stone have noted that even "noncoercive relationships require consent that is informed, mutual, and meaningful" (11). Peterson has studied the relationships of therapists and their patients, indicating, "'Informed' means that all of the possible risks and consequences have been communicated and understood. 'Mutual' means that the power in the relationship is equal. 'Meaningful' means that the patient can say no without the possibility of harmful consequences to self, the treatment, or the relationship" (124).

Clearly, such a definition of consent does not apply to the teacher and student in high school or middle school. The sexual involvement is likely illegal, based on statutory rape guidelines in the state in question, and/or contrary to school policy, with regard to the guidelines for teacher behavior, and ethically questionable, particularly for the professional whose educational preparation included the study of human development. Thus, apart from the immaturity of the young person, such relationships highlight the ethical decision making of the teacher.

Generally speaking, the research on role modeling shows that the potential for influence is great, the issue of power is at work, and the nature of decision making is potentially affected by the way in which the young person views the role model.

At the same time, decision making about relationships with adults in positions of authority is not the same as the sexual decision making of young people overall. The research on television viewing has revealed "substantial associations between the amount of sexual content viewed by adolescents and advances in their sexual behavior during the subsequent year" (Collins et al. 2004). However, while the research regarding exposure to sexually provocative lyrics "provide[s] evidence that such exposure is related to advances in a range of sexual activities among adolescents, including intercourse and noncoital behavior" (Martino et al. 2006), it also identifies "an important limitation to music effects. . . . [T]he influence of sexual music content on teens' sexual development is specific to content that is sexually degrading" (Ibid.).

Much of the research related to adolescent sexual behavior and decision making is based on concerns related to reports of earlier sexual activity among young people, the potential risks associated with sexual behavior among young people, and the desire to develop informed intervention approaches based on an understanding of the current context. A study of decision making of adolescents regarding sexual behavior, published in 2005, considered "two major decision points: whether or not to engage in sexual intercourse and whether or not to use safer sex methods" (Michels, Kropp, Eyre, and Halpern-Felsher, 584). Based on earlier findings, which "identified risk and protective factors that appear to influence adolescents' decisions to engage in sexual activity or to use safer sex methods, including self-efficacy, parental values, peer norms, supervision, decision-making orientation, and partner communication [and contextual factors, such as] adolescents' world views of permissiveness, double standards, sexual control, and romance," the researchers considered "realistic decisions, the serial nature of decision making (i.e., incorporating feedback from previous decisions into current ones), the social context in which decisions are made, and the relationship between the process of decision making and its outcome" (584–586).

Interviews with participants averaging 14.1 years old revealed examples of "a risk/benefit deliberation." The young people "sought advice from trusted friends and relatives" in "weighing the risks and benefits of each sexual situation" (593–594). However, in doing so, they were equally concerned with minimizing "health risks, especially contracting HIV," and "social risk [such as,] pregnancy and/or abortion." In other words, "[s]exually transmitted infections, while described mostly as health risks, also carried social consequences" (593). In addition, "some adolescents revealed how reflection and evaluation of past decisions influenced subsequent sexual decisions" (603). Similarly, in many instances, the young people appeared to be aware of the potential difficulty of making sound decisions in the moment, without prior preparation. In both earlier and current research, the young people prepare for sexual circumstances "by ensuring that parents or peers were nearby in situations that could lead to intercourse, considering their long-term educational and professional goals as reasons to make decisions that reduced or eliminated the possibility of pregnancy or STD transmission, considering their own religious beliefs," using "boundary setting, that is, placing a priori limits on particular sexual encounters," and "constructing boundaries first, then communicating those boundaries to potential sexual partners" (585, 595–596).

Thus, the research related to sexual decision making and adolescents reveals, along with documented pregnancy rates, disparities based on income and race, and threats associated with STDs: young people's decision making involves information gathering and use, planning, risk analysis, including the consideration of potential consequences, situation design, and boundary setting, reflecting an understanding of the difficulty of making good decisions in the moment.

In addition to the research associated with sexual decision making and the influence of authority figures in the decision making process regarding relationship formation, researchers and news organizations have addressed the impact of providing or limiting access to information and limiting choices with specific penalties, in relation to the decision making of young people. This research has addressed a range of types of decisions, including those related to sexual activity, as well as drinking, drug experimentation and use, and driving, among others.

Ethical decision making is not only the result of will and the realization of scrutiny and anticipated accountability, but also preparation for decision making. Unfortunately, neither K-12 nor higher education provides sufficient preparation for critical thinking and analytical skills. While young people attempt to develop strategies and make use of available information in response to personal challenges, employers are less than pleased with the decision making abilities they bring to the job.

REFERENCES

Barner, Robert. "Five Steps to Leadership Competencies." *Training & Development* 54(3) (March 2000): 47–51.

Beam, Margaret R., Chuansheng Chen, and Ellen Greenberger. "The Nature of Adolescents' Roles with Their 'Very Important' Nonparental Adults." *American Journal of Community Psychology* 30 (April 2002): 305–325.

Brown, William J., Michael D., Basil, and Mihai C. Bocarnea. "The Influence of Famous Athletes on Health Beliefs and Practices: Mark McGwire, Child Abuse Prevention, and Androstenedione." *Journal of Health Communication* 8 (2003): 41–57.

Collins, Rebecca L., Marc N. Elliott, Sandra H. Berry, David E. Kanouse, Dale Kunkel, Sarah B. Hunter, and Angela Miu. "Watching Sex on Television Predicts Adolescent Initiation of Sexual Behavior." *Pediatrics* 114(3) (September 2004): e280–e289. Available at http://pediatrics.aappublications.org/cgi/reprint/114/3/e280 (accessed February 3, 2008).

Gollop, Jane. *Feminist Accused of Sexual Harassment.* Durham, NC:Duke University Press, 1997.

Intagliata, Jim, Dave Ulrich, Norm Smallwood. "Leveraging Leadership Competencies to Produce Leadership Brand: Creating Distinctiveness by Focusing on Strategy and Results." *Human Resource Planning* 23(3) (2000): 12–23.

Martino, Steven C., Rebecca L. Collins, Marc N. Elliott, Amy Strachman, David E. Danouse, and Sandra H. Berry. "Exposure to Degrading Versus Nondegrading Music Lyrics and Sexual Behavior among Youth." *Pediatrics* 118(2) (August 2006): e430–e441. Available at http://pediatrics.aappublications.org/cgi/reprint/118/2/e430 (accessed February 3, 2008).

Michels, Tricia M., Rhonda Y. Kropp, Stephen L. Eyre, and Bonnie L. Halpern-Felsher. "Initiating Sexual Experiences: How Do Young Adolescents Make Decisions regarding Early Sexual Activity?" *Journal of Research on Adolescence* 15(4) (2005): 583–607.

Orr, William Alexander. *The Socialization of Prejudices.* Clinton, SC: Southern Sociological Society, 2003.

Pellegrini, Ann. "Pedagogy's Turn: Observations on Students, Teachers, and Transference-Love." *Critical Inquiry* 25 (Spring 1999): 617–625.

Peterson, Marilyn R. *At Personal Risk: Boundary Violations in Professional-Client Relationships.* New York: Norton, 1992.

Stamler, Virginia Lee, and Gerald L. Stone. *Faculty-Student Sexual Involvement.* Thousand Oaks, CA: Sage Publications, 1998.

CHAPTER 6
Civic Engagement and Access to Information

Full participation in society (and in the context of this discussion) necessarily includes participation in the political and policy making processes and in overall civic engagement. The U.S. Constitution guarantees rights associated with citizenship, as well as the concomitant responsibilities. According to constitutional scholar Jethro Lieberman, "The right to cast a ballot is—along with the First Amendment's guarantee of a right to discuss the issues—the centerpiece of American democracy" (1987, 159). Therefore, voting might be viewed as the ultimate exercise of participation in society.

While the U.S. Constitution focused primarily on questions of electing officials for national office, the constitutional basis for encouraging political participation is well documented. The democratic form of government envisioned and outlined (somewhat broadly) by the framers of the U.S. Constitution was that of a representative democracy, with citizen participation and some measure of transparency of government. However, the concept of participation in the political process is based on two premises: the opportunity to participate and informed participation. While the Constitution provided reasonable limitations on participation by members of society, with regard to eligibility for election to federal political office, it was not until the ratification of the Fifteenth Amendment in 1870 gave African Americans the right to vote, and the Nineteenth Amendment in 1920 extended the right to vote to women, that the concept of relatively universal political participation was codified.

Even so, despite the constitutional recognition and subsequent interpretation of states' rights, the Fifteenth and the Nineteenth Amendments did not prohibit individual states from implementing laws and practices that limited participation based on race and socioeconomic status. By using requirements of land ownership, poll taxes, literacy tests, and the "grandfather clause," state and local officials were able to limit voting rights to: those of financial means; those who could demonstrate—to the satisfaction of polling officials—not only literacy but also an "understanding" of the U.S. Constitution; and those whose grandfathers were eligible to vote and were, thus, not slaves. It was not until 1971 that the Twenty-Sixth Amendment "extended the franchise to all citizens at least eighteen years old," providing a constitutional basis for the provision passed in the Voting Rights Act a year earlier (Lieberman 1987, 160). The impact of the Twenty-Sixth Amendment was greater than that of codifying the principle of access to the political process for all adult U.S. citizens, save those with felony convictions. Additionally, the Amendment acknowledged the federal government's role in ensuring access to political participation, via cooperation among the three branches of government, and that such a principle was not superseded by the focus on states' rights.

This checkered past reflects an understanding of constitutional ideals of full participation by both those who encouraged and those who attempted to limit such access. Political participation represents a level of power that provides unparalleled opportunities for influence and includes activities such as voting, campaigning for political candidates, lobbying for causes of interest, supporting individuals and organizations with which one agrees politically, and volunteerism. Thus, civic engagement offers the opportunity, not only for influence in the process but also for leadership development, networking, learning, and skills development.

It is also true that informed participation goes beyond simple familiarity with current events. The U.S. political system is quite complex, in both design and operation, making full understanding difficult and political literacy less than universal, especially for young people. In providing a bit of an analysis of that complexity, a number of examples are illustrative:

- The U.S. political system is characterized by local (municipal), county, state, and federal governments, as well as quasi-governmental agencies and other agencies or functions, such as the postal service and airport security screening, which have gone from public to at least partial private control, management, and ownership.
- The political system at the federal level includes the executive, legislative, and judicial branches.
- At all levels there are issues of agency and court jurisdiction and processes to ensure the separation of powers.
- At the federal level, the popular vote and the electoral college function in combination, with the former informing but not overriding the latter.
- In the legislative branch, there are two elected U.S. Senators per state, whereas the number of U.S. Representatives is determined on a proportional basis, with different terms of office for the Representatives and Senators and no term limits, at present.
- The Office of the President has a limit of two full terms, while Supreme Court justices are appointed for life.
- The process of the appointment of federal judges and Supreme Court justices requires nomination by the executive branch and review and confirmation by the legislative branch.
- Political parties identify their leadership in the House and the Senate, while the Chief Justice is confirmed by the Congress, after being nominated by the President.
- The levels of judicial review include federal district courts, appellate courts, and the U.S. Supreme Court.
- The legislative process includes the introduction of bills, committee review, congressional hearings, voting, and reconciliation of the House and Senate versions of proposed legislation.
- With the House and Senate versions of legislation, there are also conference committees that include members from both houses.
- Some Congressional votes require a majority to pass. A so-called super majority of 60 percent (three-fifths) is required to move to a vote through a motion called a cloture—closing debate on a topic and ending a filibuster—in the Senate. And, in the other type of super majority, a two-thirds (66.7 percent) majority is required in a number of instances, most notably to override a presidential veto, and, in the most straightforward process for amending the Constitution, each House of the U.S. Congress must pass the amendment by a two-thirds vote, and then three-quarters of the state legislatures must ratify the amendment.
- The names of Congressional committees and subcommittees, with their areas of responsibility, are not intuitive. The House Committee on Ways

and Means, for example, controls some but not all revenue-generating measures, including taxation. Ways and Means is distinct from both the Budget and the Appropriations Committees. There is no Ways and Means committee in the U.S. Senate. In the Senate, the designation of "Homeland Security" was appended to the previously existing Committee on Governmental Affairs, such that the same committee oversees the National Archives and Records Administration, the U.S. Census Bureau, and antiterrorist programs.

- There is the ongoing process of interpretation of constitutional intent and legislative intent, in the context of the exercise of executive powers, regulation, and oversight.
- The constitutional basis for governmental structure and separation of powers includes relatively explicit explanation of intent in some cases and ongoing interpretations in others, evolving in some circumstances, including the move from the original Department of War to the current Department of State, for example.
- U.S. Congressional districts vary in size and configuration by state, and based on the 2006 Supreme Court decision, they may be reconfigured at times other than following the release of census results.
- State, local, and county governments vary in structure, with appointed and elected positions, mayors, governors, city and town councils, city and county commissioners, city managers, county executives, and varying terms and election guidelines.
- Election cycles vary. And, ballots may include national candidates, as well as candidates and ballot questions at the state, county, and local levels.
- The system includes complex legal and tax codes that vary by level of government.
- The appropriations process includes the combination of local, state, and federal funding received by public agencies, such as libraries, public universities, and K-12 school systems.
- There is the confusing circumstance of the missions of federal agencies. In the investigatory realm, the roles of the U.S. Department of Justice, CIA, FBI, NSA, Department of Homeland Security, Bureau of Alcohol, Tobacco, and Firearms, Government Accountability Office, Federal Aviation Administration, and Federal Trade Commission, among others, may not be easily understood and discerned.

Thus, in light of the issues of fostering both interest and understanding, there are local and national efforts to demystify the political process and to encourage young people in particular to become informed and engaged.

As cochair of the National Advisory Council of the Campaign for the Civic Mission of Schools, former Supreme Court Justice Sandra Day O'Connor has endorsed the organization's goals "to improve and expand civic learning in our schools." Based on the realization that quality education in this area is important, the organization supports enhanced "professional development [for teachers] in the area of civic education" (Skaggs and Conrad 2006, C.13). With her cochair, former governor of Colorado and Los Angeles superintendent of schools Roy Romer, "they are reminding us that democracy, representative government and the rule of law don't just happen; they take work—and the understanding that the public schools must provide" (Broder 2006, B.07).

Similarly, a number of other organizations which are national with local affiliates have as their missions the enhancement of democracy and increased education and involvement in the political and civic processes. For example, "[t]he League of Women Voters, a nonpartisan political organization, has fought since 1920 to improve our systems of government and impact public policies through citizen education and advocacy. . . . The organization remains true to its basic purpose: to make democracy work for all citizens."

A statement of the NAACP Legal Defense Fund indicates, "We believe that quality education, health care, meaningful employment and economic opportunities, the right to vote and fully participate in democracy, and the right to a fair and just judicial system, especially as applied to criminal proceedings, are fundamental and basic human rights."

In addition, according to the Young Democrats of America, "[o]pen to anyone under the age of 36 who affiliates with the Democratic Party, YDA is a nationwide grassroots organization with 42 chartered states and 780 local chapters. . . . All of the members have the interest of their community at heart and work hard to affect the democratic process. YDA works hard to:

- Elect Democratic Candidates
- Encourage youth involvement in the Democratic Party
- Support the ideals of the Democratic Party at all levels of government

- Instill young people with the values for which the Democratic Party stands
- Provide young people with the skills and experiences they will need to lead our nation"

And, the Article 2 Statement of Purpose of the Young Republican National Federation indicates that "[t]he purpose of the YRNF is to develop a nationwide movement of intelligent, aggressive, professional and effective Young Republicans through education and training."

However, there are a number of other organizations that focus on active encouragement of civic engagement by young people. The conservative John W. Pope Civitas Institute, which is affiliated with the John Locke Foundation, provides leadership training institutes and focuses on preparing young people to participate in the political process. Similarly, since its founding in 1970, the Close Up Foundation is "the nation's largest nonprofit . . . , nonpartisan citizenship education organization," and has worked with more than 600,000 participants "to promote responsible and informed participation in the democratic process through" (Close Up Foundation, "About Us") "civic education programs [for] middle schoolers, high schoolers, and adults," particularly teachers (Close Up Foundation, Mission, Vision and Beliefs).

Finally, the Coalition of Community Foundations for Youth is a collaborative charity organization that provides grant funding and technical assistance to member organizations which address various issues related to young people. Its extensive civic engagement component for youth fosters interest in and preparation for active and informed civic engagement.

As a result of the fact that, in some instances, these organizations are partisan or otherwise reflective of political or philosophical agendas, young people need to be discerning. The reach, membership, and influence of these organizations are relatively limited; plus the Internet and increased exposure to civics education hold promise for enhanced interest and participation for young people in the political process. In addition, the public library as an institution has been described as the "people's university," with the role of fostering access to information and the principles of intellectual freedom, in encouraging the development of an informed citizenry, in a nonpartisan context.

However, civic engagement requires both interest in and a basis for sound decision making, in an understanding of the issues and the political process. As the majority of the political impediments to full participation have been removed, limitations on access to information continue. The ability to participate in an informed way is limited by one's access to information, as well as one's ability to synthesize and make use of that information in the decision making process. These limitations are dependent on the degree of literacy, in general, as well as what has been termed information literacy (the ability to conduct research, locate, and evaluate information), broad analytical and critical thinking skills, and media literacy (representative of the extent to which much of the information related to the political process is made available via the print, broadcast, and online media). Unfortunately, while access to media outlets and Internet resources is key, it is often limited by socioeconomic status, including the level of access in rural and urban school systems.

There is also the concept of political literacy, which reflects both the complexity of the U.S. political system and the calls by leaders, including Sandra Day O'Connor of the Campaign for the Civic Mission of Schools, to ensure academic preparation for young people. Clearly, the challenges associated with academic preparation include balancing civic curricula with that in other areas; addressing the issue of local and state academic guidelines and requirements; and, fostering a culture of civics education among teachers, administrators, school boards, and Departments of Education. Even so, "[w]hile the decline in civic engagement over the past 30 years is evident among all age groups, it is particularly acute among the young. Put simply, America's youth appear to be disconnecting from public life, and [are] doing so at a rate that is greater than any other age group" (Carpini 2000). Conversely, some refer to "the gap between declining political participation and high levels of political interest by young people" (O'Toole, Marsh, and Jones 2003, 349), such that examples of volunteerism and other forms of engagement show an entirely different trend.

A key measure of civic engagement is voting by young people, whether those who are eighteen to twenty-four years of age or those in their mid-thirties. For the most part, there has been "a steady decrease in turnout" in the last thirty years (Lopez, Kirby, and Sagoff 2005, 4), with two exceptions: a "spike" in voter turnout of young people in

1992; and a corresponding increase in 2004. It is not clear whether the 2004 increase represents a new direction or the result of "confluence of extensive voter outreach efforts, a close election, and high levels of interest in the 2004 campaign" (Ibid., 1). While there is evidence of campaigners' actively targeting young people for 2008 (Cassata 2004), a number of analyses of voter turnout among young people however suggest the unique circumstance of a high level of interest in the 2004 election cycle. As a researcher has noted, "[T]he extraordinary events from the disputed outcome of the 2000 race, to the tragedy of September 11th, to the invasions of Afghanistan and Iraq [indicate] . . . that the period leading up to Election Day 2004 was no ordinary time" (Wattenberg 2005, 145). Another analyst has made reference to additional issues at the time, including "the economy particularly, and to a polarizing president." (Patterson 2004) However, the researchers suggest that in the absence of a similar set of motivating issues, "it is uncertain whether young adults will again flock to the polls" (Ibid.).

In this regard, the results of a longitudinal research study at UCLA, from the mid-1960s and involving 250,000 matriculating college freshmen each year, show that "every significant indicator of political engagement has fallen by about half." The research further says, "Only 33% of freshmen think that keeping up with politics is important, down from 60% in 1966. . . . Only 16% say they frequently discuss politics, down from 33% in 1966" (Galston 2003, 30).

Still, "[a]s far back as evidence can be found—and virtually without exception—young adults seem to have been less attached to civic life than their parents and grandparents" (Ibid., 29). However, with increasing personal development and putting down roots, "in every generation the simple passage of time has brought maturing young adults more fully into the circle of civic life" (Ibid.).

And, for the most part, "[t]oday's young people are patriotic, tolerant, and compassionate. They believe in America's principles and in the American Dream. They adeptly navigate our nation's increasing diversity. And, as has been widely reported and discussed, they are more than willing to give of themselves to others" (Ibid., 30). However, is there evidence that volunteerism will lead to wider civic engagement? For certain, it is an important component of civic engagement in the minds of young people, who "typically characterize their volunteering as an *alternative* to official politics, which they see as self-absorbed and unrelated to their deeper ideals" (Ibid.). In this regard, young people appear to see greater potential for their individual acts of service than those of the government; in fact, the majority of those under thirty (56 percent), even more so for those under twenty-five (60 percent) "believe that government should do more to solve problems" (Youth Voting 2005).

Particularly during the 2004 presidential primary season, the organization MoveOn.org was lauded for its success in fostering interest and engagement in the campaign and the political process. While the source of the group's success in encouraging the involvement of young people is not completely clear, possible explanations include: the use of the Internet and communication technology in disseminating its messages and encouraging participation; political agendas of interest to some young people; and marketing to, recruitment of, and exhibition of interest in this specific audience.

How the population of "young people" is defined may vary from those in K-12 education, college students and others in their late teens and early twenties, to young workers. Generation X, as a segment of the population, is generally defined as those born from the mid to late 1960s through the 1970s. While Generation X has been characterized as disillusioned, less engaged, and independent, the focus on sound decision making and full participation in society should be informed by more than the generalizations regarding the sociological characteristics that have been attributed to a generation. There is the need for a more substantive analysis of this segment of the population.

Why then do young people display a lack of engagement overall and/or interest in politics, in particular? "According to media rhetoric, the majority of Generation X wants little to do with government, is selfish, lazy and shuns civic responsibilities and commitments. As a testament to these notions, GenXers have inherited several nicknames, among them, *Slacker Generation* and *The Me Generation*" (Crowley 2003). This group also tends to be characterized negatively in relation to prior generations. "Popular literature along with a multitude of research studies conducted depicts the children born to 'Baby Boomers' (Generation Xers) as the most cynical and detached of current generations" (Ibid.).

Research regarding Generation X has found that "[s]kepticism and mistrust towards the government is pervasive among this group of respondents. Respondents' past negative experiences and interactions with federal bureaucracies do influence their overall negative attitudes toward government" (de la Puente 2004, 1). In particular, after including "'hard to reach' respondent populations, such as ethnic minorities, lower socioeconomic classes, immigrants and alienated young adults," it was discovered that "[m]inority Generation X respondents . . . generally did not confirm many of the negative stereotypes (e.g., selfishness, detached from civic responsibility) that surround all Generation X cohort members." Thus, while Generation X, in general, may not possess all of the qualities attributed to it, there are substantial distinctions within the segment of the population.

To the extent that there is some disillusionment among the young, the reasons for it are worth considering. With regard to the political process, the likelihood of disillusionment is related to the contentious and partisan political environment, as well as the numerous ethical scandals of elected officials and other leaders and a sense of powerlessness in affecting the process and the outcome. In an article entitled "A Politics for Generation X," Ted Halstead suggests that "the distinction between Democrats and Republicans, which has defined American politics for more than a century, doesn't resonate much with the young, who tend to see more similarities than differences between the two parties." Such feelings and perceptions appear to lead to apathy, as well as a sense that "Xers have internalized [a number of] core beliefs," including the sense that they are "more likely to describe [themselves] as having a negative attitude toward America, and as placing little importance on citizenship and national identity." There is the related reality of perception of "a more materialistic and individualistic streak" (1999, 34). In addition, political participation includes the potential for being tied to a specific political or philosophical agenda or partisan label. Such a challenge to one's independence is not likely to be welcomed by those who value independence and autonomy and who may question authority more generally.

Concerning access to information related to the political process and political issues, young people's lack of interest in the political process is seemingly reflected in an overall lack of exposure to news and current events, at least from traditional news sources. According to the results of a 2006 survey published in *The Wall Street Journal*, "46% of students (down from 49% last year) read the print version of at least one national newspaper in a typical week," as compared with "71% of college students [who] read at least one of the last five issues of the college paper" (Steel 2006, B1). While there is always the potential for a "positive response" bias with self-report research regarding an activity that individuals may assume they should engage in (i.e., reading the newspaper), these results indicate quite clearly that college students prefer getting their news from a campus newspaper than from a national newspaper.

Similarly, the median age for broadcast news audiences, both network and cable, is well over the age of fifty, suggesting limited viewership among young people. Specifically, with regard to network news, "In fall 2003, the median age for the three network evening news programs ranged from 59.5 for ABC to 60.3 for NBC to 61.2 for CBS, slightly older than cable." In terms of cable news, "the median age for CNN viewers is 59.6; for Fox News it is 58.3, and for MSNBC it is 52.4" (Journalism.org, 2004). Limited time slots and program length may explain a disadvantage for broadcast news over cable or online news. However, until 2006, the Nielsen ratings had not included college students living in separate households (Aspan 2006), such that our knowledge of the group must often be extrapolated from other studies.

Television Week writer Michael Levine has noted that young people's limited viewing and reading of traditional sources of news and political information is accompanied by skepticism about politicians and politics. "Young people, especially, have become increasingly wary of the political process and the people who participate in it," he claims. "Quite often their chief source of information can be from a Web site whose point of view is slanted to either side of the political spectrum" (2006, 14).

So, which sources of news and information do young people consult? Research suggests a high percentage of college students are viewers of Jon Stewart's television program, *The Daily Show*, and has begun to document and measure what has been called "*The Daily Show* effect." It appears that young people who are regular viewers of this political satire "exhibit more cynicism toward the electoral system and the news media at large" (Baumgartner and Morris 2006, 341). On the pro side, so-called soft news is shown to "contribute to democratic citizenship in America by reaching out to the inattentive public" (Ibid.).

Conversely, "*The Daily Show* effect" appears to "have more detrimental effects, driving down support for political institutions and leaders among those already inclined toward nonparticipation" (Ibid.). More specifically, "exposure to *The Daily Show* negatively correlates with faith in the electoral system and assessments of the media's political coverage.... [F]or young people, no other news source drives cynicism toward the candidates and the political system more than *The Daily Show*" (Ibid., 359).

In an article entitled "Nothing Wrong with Healthy Skepticism," Levine "reflects" on such research and the suggested impact of *The Daily Show* and political satire, in general, on the political opinions of young U.S. viewers. He indicates, "It is said that the show makes fun of the media and politicians" (2006, 14). However, while Levine acknowledges the level of cynicism among young people, he questions the sources of such feelings: "So, it's *The Daily Show*, and not real-life events, that makes young people cynical about politics?" (Ibid.). The low levels of viewership and readership of traditional sources of news and political information suggest that "[p]eople will not pay attention to things that don't interest them.... Until those nuggets of information are made human and accessible, people won't take action in any direction politically" (Ibid.).

Suggesting that the combination of information and humor may serve to foster greater interest and scrutiny of politicians, he notes the potential for a "positive effect of the show on the ability of young viewers to converse casually on such issues as gay marriage and the nation's reliance on foreign energy" (Ibid.). The nature of satire is such that it requires both an ability to scrutinize and discern humor and sarcasm and also the desire to supplement the information presented. Levine has noted, "[I]f the viewer is interested, he can certainly find more legitimate news sources (we are awash in news sources in the 21st Century) that will provide information without jokes" (Ibid.).

Certainly, the sources of news and political information to which young people have access are many and varied. In some instances, these organizations offer information that is partisan, reflective of particular political or philosophical agendas, or satirical. Despite a lack of reverence, soft news sources may well foster greater interest in and scrutiny of politicians and encourage democratic citizenship. Michael

Levine suggests, "[It may be] that they are more engaged, not less. I believe that they are at least questioning the process and that means that they are interested in the process" (Ibid.). If so, the question becomes how to ensure that that interest and this type of engagement actually lead to active and involved political participation.

Unfortunately, the nature of current civics education is disappointing. Researcher William Galston has noted that "[t]he evidence that we have failed to transmit basic civil knowledge to young adults is not incontrovertible" (2003, 31). Civics education is in competition with academic curricula in areas such as math and science. And, unlike other aspects of the curriculum, there is the concern among educators, administrators, and "school boards [which] fear criticism—or even litigation—if they address topics some parents or other members of the community may consider inappropriate" (Ibid., 32). However, the results of testing indicate that in this area "student performance is quite low" (Ibid.).

This state of affairs is unfortunate because of the potential for civic education for individuals and society. Galston for one claims that:

Civic knowledge promotes support for democratic values. . . . Civic knowledge helps citizens to understand their interests as individuals and as members of groups. . . . The more knowledge we have of public affairs, the less we have a sort of generalized mistrust and fear of public life. . . . Civic knowledge improves the consistency of citizens' views as expressed in public opinion surveys. . . . Civic knowledge can alter our opinion on specific civic issues. (32–33)

Education then has the potential, not only to enhance collective knowledge regarding the nature of the complexity of political issues and the political process, but also to foster interest in civic engagement, enhancing the level of interest and informed participation.

More broadly, the nature of the individual and societal issues facing young people represent a challenging decision making circumstance. Whether the issues are academic, professional, political, or sexual, there is evidence that young people seek information and guidance and attempt to make good decisions, at least in some instances. Thus, education provides them a basis for enhancing the decision making process and encouraging full participation, whether in leadership roles or in their own lives. The circumstance of ethical issues in particular indicates the competing motivations, the complexity associated with ethical decision making, and the fact that ethical decision making requires informed preparation.

The founding principles of the United States reflect the importance of education for its own sake and for its role in preparing individuals for the responsibilities associated with full participation in society. The founders articulated these principles two hundred and thirty-one years ago, with little conception of the ways in which society would change and diversify. However, they defined a societal ideal that was based upon principles that required full participation for the society to prosper. In 1954, the Supreme Court addressed the importance of access to education as necessary in support of full participation in society. Certainly, enhanced preparation in the use of information in support of decision making, in terms of analytical and critical thinking skills, information literacy, media literacy, and political literacy requires a societal commitment to preparing people for leadership roles and a collective sense that their full participation in society is important.

REFERENCES

Aspan, Maria. "Nielsen Will Start to Measure TV Habits of College Students." *The New York Times* (February 20, 2006). Available at http://www.nytimes.com/2006/02/20/business/media/20nielsen.html?ex=1298091600&en=1f16787e644d9d08&ei=5090&partner=rssuserland&emc=rss (accessed September 18, 2006).

Baumgartner, Jody, and Jonathan S. Morris. "*The Daily Show* Effect: Candidate Evaluations, Efficacy, and American Youth." *American Politics Research* 43 (May 2006): 341–367.

Broder, David S. "Saving Democracy, Pupil by Pupil." *The Washington Post* (April 23, 2006): B.07.

Carpini, Michael X. Delli. "Gen.com: Youth Civic Engagement, and the New Information Environment." *Political Communication* 17 (October–December 2000): 341–349.

Cassata, Donna. "Voter Turnout among the Young Still Lags." *USA Today* (March 4, 2004). Available at http://www.usatoday.com/news/elections/2007-03-04-787496319_x.htm (accessed April 25, 2007).

Close Up Foundation. "About Us." Available at http://www.closeup.org/aboutcuf.htm (accessed February 3, 2008).

———. "Mission, Vision and Beliefs." Available at http://www.closeup.org/mission.htm#mission (accessed April 18, 2006).

Coalition of Community Foundations for Youth. "About CCFY." Available at http://www.ccfy.org/aboutus/index.htm (accessed April 18, 2006).

———. "Youth Civic Engagement." Available at http://www.ccfy.org/civic/index.htm (accessed April 18, 2006).

"Constitution of the Young Republican National Federation, Inc." Available at http://www.yrnf.com/docs/governing/YRNFConstitution_2007.pdf (accessed February 2, 2008).

Crowley, Melinda. *Generation X Speaks Out on Civic Engagement and the Decennial Census: An Ethnographic Approach.* June 17, 2003. http://www.census.gov/pred/www/rpts/Generation%20X%20Final%20Report.pdf (accessed February 3, 2008).

Galston, William A. "Civic Education and Political Participation." *Phi Delta Kappan* 84(1) (September 2003): 29–33.

Halstead, Ted. "A Politics for Generation X." *Atlantic Monthly* 284 (2) (August 1999): 33–42.

Journalism.org. "The State of the News Media 2004: An Annual Report on American Journalism." State of the News Media. 2004. Available at http://www.stateofthenewsmedia.org/narrative_cabletv_audience.asp?media=5&cat=3 (accessed August 30, 2006).

League of Women Voters. "About the League." Available at http://www.lwv.org/AM/Template.cfm?Section=About_Us (accessed February 2, 2008).

Levine, Michael. "Nothing Wrong with Healthy Skepticism." *Television Week* (July 12, 2006): 14.

Lieberman, Jethro K. *The Enduring Constitution: A Bicentennial Perspective* St. Paul, MN: West Publishing Company, 1987.

Lopez, Mark Hugo, Emily Kirby, and Jared Sagoff. *CIRCLE (The Center for Information & Research on Civic Learning & Engagement): The Youth Vote 2004*, 2005.

O'Toole, Therese, David Marsh, and Su Jones. "Political Literacy Cuts Both Ways: The Politics of Non-Participation Among Young People." *The Political Quarterly* 74 (July–September 2003): 349–360.

Patterson, Thomas E. *Young Voters and the 2004 Election*. Cambridge: John F. Kennedy School of Government, 2004: 7. Available at http://www.ksg.harvard.edu.libproxy.lib.unc.edu/presspol/vanishvoter/Releases/Vanishing_Voter_Final_Report_2004_Election.pdf (accessed April 24, 2007).

"President's Welcome to The NAACP Legal Defense Fund." Available at http://www.naacpldf.org/content.aspx?article=328 (accessed August 22, 2006).

Puente, Manuel de la. *Census 2000 Testing, Experimentation, and Evaluation Program Topic Report No. 15, TR-15, Census 2000 Ethnographic Studies*. Washington: U.S. Census Bureau, 2004: 1. Available at http://www.census.gov/pred/www/rpts/TR15.pdf (accessed April 24, 2007).

Skaggs, David, and Jill Conrad. "The Value of Civic Education." *The Denver Post* (March 18, 2006): C.13.

Steel, Emily. "Big Media on Campus." *The Wall Street Journal* (August 9, 2006): B1. Available at http://online.wsj.com/public/article/SB115509164245730752-UiWPbJ5AuldoE29nbxN620kcu9c_20070808.html?mod=rss_free (accessed August 28, 2006).

Wattenberg, Martin P. "Elections: Turnout in the 2004 Presidential Election." *Presidential Studies Quarterly* 35 (March 2005): 145.

Young Democrats of America. "Goals and Vision." Available at http://www.yda.org/.

Youth Voting in the 2004 Election: The Staff of the Center for Information and Research on Civic Learning and Engagement. *Social Education* 69 (January–February 2005): 33–35.

Index

About the Author

MARK WINSTON is an Associate Professor at the University of North Carolina at Chapel Hill, School of Information and Library Science. He joined the UNC faculty after nearly eight years on the faculty of Rutgers University. He is a past winner of the Literati Network Award of Excellence and has received awards for his research from the American Library Association and Reference Services Press. He conducts research in the areas of information ethics and information policy, leadership education, leadership development, leadership diversity theory, and ethical leadership. His publications include *Leadership in the Library and Information Science Professions: Theory and Practice* and *Managing Multiculturalism and Diversity in the Library: Principles and Issues for Administrators*, as well as more than thirty-five articles and chapters in various other publications. He has served on the editorial boards of the *Journal of Library and Information Science, Library Administration and Management,* and *College and Research Libraries.* He has served as a consultant and trainer for college, university, and public libraries, information technology and publishing companies, among other organizations. His doctorate and master's degrees are from the University of Pittsburgh.